Macmillan
ENCYCLOPEDIA
OF SCIENCE

11

Communication
Print, Images, Sounds, and the Computer

Rhys Lewis

Macmillan Publishing Company
New York

Maxwell Macmillan International Publishing Group
New York   Oxford   Singapore   Sydney

Board of Advisors

Linda K. Baloun, B.S., Science Teacher, Highmore, SD

Merriley Borell, Ph.D., Consultant, Contemporary Issues in Science and Medicine, Piedmont, CA

Maura C. Flannery, Ph.D., Associate Professor of Biology, St. John's University, Jamaica, NY

Owen Gingerich, Ph.D., Professor of Astronomy and History of Science, Harvard-Smithsonian Center for Astrophysics, Cambridge, MA

MaryLouise Kleman, M.A., Science Teacher, Baltimore County, MD

Irwin Tobias, Ph.D., Professor of Chemistry, Rutgers University, New Brunswick, NJ

Bibliographer

Sondra F. Nachbar, M.L.S., Librarian-in-Charge, The Bronx High School of Science, Bronx, NY

Advisory Series Editor

Robin Kerrod

Consultant

Dr. J. Beynon

U.S. Editorial and Design Staff

Jean Paradise, Editorial Director
Richard Hantula, Senior Editor
Mary Albanese, Design Director
Zelda Haber, Design Consultant
Norman Dane, Cover Design

Andromeda Staff

Caroline Sheldrick, Editor
David West/Children's Book Design, Designer
Alison Renney, Picture Research
Steve Elliott, Production
John Ridgeway, Art Director
Lawrence Clarke, Project Director

Front Cover: Cyber 205 supercomputer, rear view
(Rainbow/Hank Morgan)

Published by:
Macmillan Publishing Company
A Division of Macmillan, Inc.
866 Third Avenue, New York, NY 10022

Collier Macmillan Canada, Inc.
1200 Eglinton Avenue East, Suite 200
Don Mills, Ontario M3C 3N1

Planned and produced by Andromeda Oxford Ltd.

Copyright © 1991 Andromeda Oxford Ltd.
Macmillan edition copyright © 1991 Macmillan Publishing Company

Library of Congress Cataloging-in-Publication Data

Macmillan encyclopedia of science.
         p.   cm.
     Includes bibliographical references and index.
     Summary: An encyclopedia of science and technology, covering such areas as the Earth, the ocean, plants and animals, medicine, agriculture, manufacturing, and transportation.
     ISBN 0-02-941346-X (set)
     1. Science–Encyclopedias, Juvenile.   2. Engineering–Encyclopedias, Juvenile.   3. Technology–Encyclopedias, Juvenile.
     [1. Science–Encyclopedias.   2. Technology–Encyclopedias.]
     I. Macmillan Publishing Company   90-19940
     Q121.M27   1991   CIP
     503 – dc20   AC

Volumes of the *Macmillan Encyclopedia of Science*
 1 *Matter and Energy* ISBN 0-02-941141-6
 2 *The Heavens* ISBN 0-02-941142-4
 3 *The Earth* ISBN 0-02-941143-2
 4 *Life on Earth* ISBN 0-02-941144-0
 5 *Plants and Animals* ISBN 0-02-941145-9
 6 *Body and Health* ISBN 0-02-941146-7
 7 *The Environment* ISBN 0-02-941147-5
 8 *Industry* ISBN 0-02-941341-9
 9 *Fuel and Power* ISBN 0-02-941342-7
10 *Transportation* ISBN 0-02-941343-5
11 *Communication* ISBN 0-02-941344-3
12 *Tools and Tomorrow* ISBN 0-02-941345-1

Printed in the United States of America

Introduction

This volume explores the diverse communication methods available today. Some, such as electronic mail, depend for their very existence on modern inventions like the computer. Even such an old method as printing has benefited from the use of computers. The second half of the volume takes a close look at computers and their uses.

To learn about a specific topic, start by consulting the Index at the end of the book. You can find references throughout the encyclopedia to the topic by turning to the final Index, covering all 12 volumes, located in Volume 12.

If you come across an unfamiliar word while using this book, the Glossary may be of help. A list of key abbreviations can be found on page 87. If you want to learn more about the subjects covered in the book, the Further Reading section is a good place to begin.

Scientists tend to express measurements in units belonging to the "International System," which incorporates metric units. This encyclopedia accordingly uses metric units (with American equivalents also given in the main text). More information on units of measurement is on page 86.

Contents

Part One

Print, images, sounds

Communication is as old as the human race. Even before there were recognizable languages, people made sounds and signs to talk to one another. The invention of efficient printing methods in the 1400s allowed people to publish their views and distribute them widely. Since the 1800s there have been great advances in communication technology. First the telegraph and then the telephone put people in touch with one another across cities and continents. Radio became the first means of mass sound communication. Millions of people could be reached in their own homes by broadcasts transmitted from a central studio. In the second half of our century, television has overtaken radio as the main broadcasting medium. Today our planet is circled by satellites high above its surface. They instantly relay telephone calls, television pictures, and other forms of electronic communication.

◄ Compact disks store sound in digital form. They are very accurate and long-lasting. The plastic material is coated with aluminum and then with lacquer for extra protection.

The printed word

▶ Each copy of this book contains identical reproductions of the original pictures chosen to illustrate the subjects. As you read this book, other people all around the world can read the same book printed in their own language.

Every day we are all surrounded by print in newspapers, magazines, books, maps, posters, and countless other things. Printing allows words and pictures to be set down and copied at great speed. It has increased enormously the amount of information that we can now share about our world.

Many thousands of copies of this book have been printed. The words and pictures in the book have to be prepared for printing in different ways and then brought together for the print run to produce the finished book. Color pictures are printed four times, each time in a different-colored ink. Similar processes are used for all printed work. Many newspapers are now produced by the most advanced printing methods, using computers and lasers, and include color pictures.

Typesetting

To print a page of a book, a copy of the words first has to be made out of metal. The completed metal letter will be covered in ink, and pieces of paper will be pressed against it to transfer the ink to the page. The traditional way to produce the printed page is for a typesetter to select individual metal letters, each made as a mirror image of the letter to be printed. The case in which all the metal letters are stored has the capital letters in the upper part and the small letters in the lower part. This is why they are sometimes called uppercase and lowercase letters. The metal pieces are picked from the case and the typesetter arranges them in order, upside down in a hand-held composing stick.

When the row of letters is complete, it is positioned as the bottom line on a frame called a galley. When the next line is complete, it is set above the previous line. The whole page is built up in this way. The finished galley contains an upside-down copy of the original page as it would appear in a mirror. When this is inked and used to print from, the printed page has the lines in the right order and all the letters the right way around.

Modern methods of typesetting avoid the lengthy process of arranging each metal letter individually. The author's writing can be typed into a word processor and stored on a computer disk. The completed disk is then given to the compositor, whose job is to translate the required page layout into computer commands on the disk. This will include details of the line length, spacing between lines, the typeface to be used, and the arrangement of the text on the page. Spaces will be left for pictures to be inserted later.

All these features of the finished page can be finalized on the computer screen without anything having to be printed. When the page of text is complete, the disk is transferred to a machine called a phototypesetter, which produces a copy of the finalized text in the correct position on transparent film. The shapes of all the letters are stored in the memory of the phototypesetter computer. A cathode-ray tube or a laser is used to transfer the shapes of the required letters to the film. This film is used in the manufacture of the metal printing plate, from which the paper page is printed.

▶ Traditional typesetting, which involves assembling lines of metal characters by hand. Many different styles of type are stored in the bench racks and drawers.

▼ Modern typesetting, which allows editors to change the text and decide on page layout on a computer screen. Phototypesetting machines can then set the type on film at 1,000 lines per minute.

Preparing the film

Illustrations as well as text are copied onto film, from which a printing plate can be made. Modern methods of phototypesetting can produce the film of the finished text directly. Otherwise the text is typeset in the traditional way and, after it is corrected, a photograph is taken of the printed page.

Black-and-white pictures are reproduced every day in newspapers. They appear to be accurate copies of the original, but in fact the printing process used for newspapers cannot print in gray, only in black. All the gray areas in the picture are made up of black dots on a white background (for light gray) or white dots on a black background (for dark gray). The original picture is converted to dots by photographing it through a screen containing many thousands of small holes. This screened photograph is used to make the printing plate.

Full-color pictures are printed using only black and three colors: yellow, cyan (a light blue), and magenta (a light purple), but the printed pictures you can see appear to contain all shades of color. This may be achieved by photographing the original three times through red, green, and blue colored filters. A screened copy of each photograph is then produced as for black-and-white photographs. Alternatively, the four images (for black and three colors) may be made by an electronic color scanner.

▲ Many newspapers use advanced technology to speed communication. By keeping words, illustrations, and photographs stored in a computer, they can be used as required by journalists, editors, designers, and printers. Journalists can type their stories directly into the computer. Photographs can also be scanned and entered into the computer. Editors design the layouts of the pages on screen. The finished design can then be typeset and made into film, from which printing plates are made.

▶ All printed full-color pictures are made up of three colored images, one in each of the three colors yellow, magenta, and cyan. There is also a black image. These images, when put together, make a full-color picture. In one method, the full-color original is photographed in black and white through a green filter. The resulting picture is rephotographed and screened into dots. From this a printing plate is made to be used with magenta-colored ink. Similarly, using a red filter results in the printing plate for cyan ink, and a blue filter is used for yellow ink. To print a full-color picture the paper must undergo four printing processes, one for each colored ink and one for black ink. The resulting image will be a full-color picture.

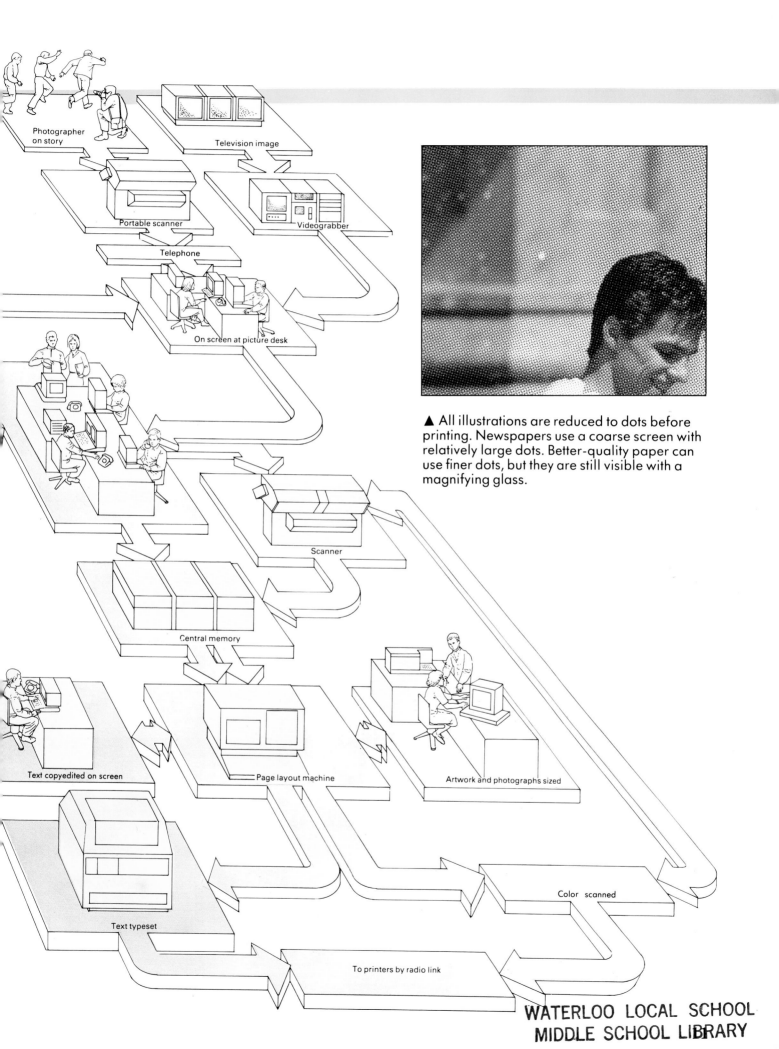

Photographer on story

Television image

Portable scanner

Videograbber

Telephone

On screen at picture desk

Scanner

Central memory

Text copyedited on screen

Page layout machine

Artwork and photographs sized

Text typeset

Color scanned

To printers by radio link

▲ All illustrations are reduced to dots before printing. Newspapers use a coarse screen with relatively large dots. Better-quality paper can use finer dots, but they are still visible with a magnifying glass.

Printing methods

When the text has been typeset and pictures have been screened and made into final film, it is time to make the printing plate from which multiple copies will be made. All printing processes have to be designed to put ink on the paper in the places where it is required and nowhere else. There are three major printing processes, using different techniques to achieve this. These processes are called letterpress, gravure, and offset lithography. Newspapers are printed by offset lithography. Color supplements are printed by gravure.

Although the printing plates for these processes are different, they are all made in a similar way. A metal plate is covered in a light-sensitive chemical. The transparent film of the page layout is brought close to the plate, and a bright light is shined through the film onto the plate. The chemical reacts where it is exposed to the light, and in those areas it binds to the metal, acting as a protective layer on the surface. The metal is then exposed to a chemical process which either removes unprotected metal or changes its surface properties. In both cases the protective layer shields some areas of the metal from attack. The finished printing plates are wrapped around cylinders, which rotate as paper is pulled over them, transferring ink to the paper. A fourth method, silk-screen printing, is often used for posters.

Gutenberg

Although books were being printed in China over a thousand years ago, the credit for introducing mass-production printing into Europe must go to Johannes Gutenberg. He lived in Mainz in Germany in the 1400s. To print a page, the type was placed in a sliding tray and inked. The paper was placed on top, and the press was screwed down. This printing technique remained unchanged for three hundred years until rotating printing presses were invented.

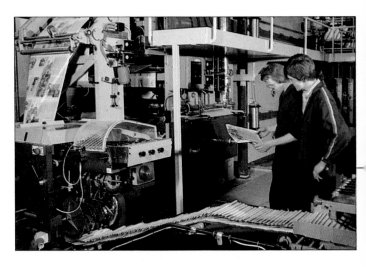

▲ A web offset press prints a continuous roll of paper.

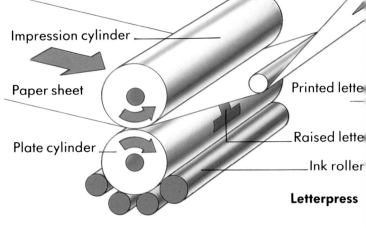

Impression cylinder

Paper sheet

Plate cylinder

Printed letter

Raised letter

Ink roller

Letterpress

▲ The letterpress method is to etch away from the printing plate those areas which should not be printed. The raised areas are inked and the plate is rolled over the paper.

Ink consists of pigments, which form the color, and additives, which control properties such as the stickiness or drying speed. A letterpress ink should be tacky and not flow very easily. In the gravure process, the ink must be thin enough to fill all the tiny cavities in the printing plate. It must also be sticky enough so that the ink is pulled out of the cavities when the paper is pressed against the plate. Lithography involves distinguishing between areas of the plate that receive ink and others which are wetted and repel ink. The ink must not run into the water but must fill all the unwetted areas. In all high-speed printing processes, ink needs to dry on the paper quickly.

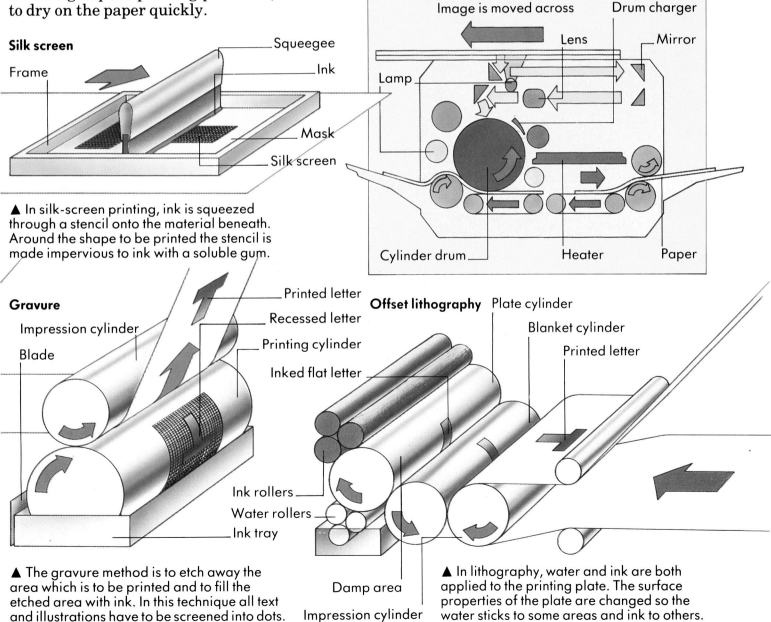

Photocopying machine

The page to be copied is placed in the machine on a transparent surface. A rotating cylinder is first given a uniform electric charge. A bright light is moved beneath the original, and an image of the page is projected onto the cylinder. Charge leaks away from those areas illuminated. A fine black powder is then sprinkled over the cylinder and is attracted to those areas still charged (the black areas). A blank piece of paper is moved over the cylinder, picking up the black powder. Heat then seals the powder on the page.

Image is moved across — Drum charger — Lens — Mirror — Lamp — Cylinder drum — Heater — Paper

Silk screen

Frame — Squeegee — Ink — Mask — Silk screen

▲ In silk-screen printing, ink is squeezed through a stencil onto the material beneath. Around the shape to be printed the stencil is made impervious to ink with a soluble gum.

Gravure

Impression cylinder — Blade — Printed letter — Recessed letter — Printing cylinder — Inked flat letter — Ink rollers — Water rollers — Ink tray

▲ The gravure method is to etch away the area which is to be printed and to fill the etched area with ink. In this technique all text and illustrations have to be screened into dots.

Offset lithography

Plate cylinder — Blanket cylinder — Printed letter — Damp area — Impression cylinder

▲ In lithography, water and ink are both applied to the printing plate. The surface properties of the plate are changed so the water sticks to some areas and ink to others.

Photography

Spot facts

• The finest microfiche is able to display up to 6,000 frames on a single sheet 10 cm (4 in.) by 15 cm (6 in.). The whole telephone directory for a large city can be stored on one sheet.

• The fastest camera in the world is used in laser research at the Blackett Laboratory in London. It is able to take up to 33 billion images per second.

• The oldest surviving color photograph was taken in 1877.

• Twinkling stars which appear white to the naked eye can be seen in full color by means of long-exposure astrophotography.

• The original daguerreotypes needed up to 20 minutes' exposure in strong sunlight, but the film in a modern pocket camera is 36,000 times as fast, with an exposure time of only 1/30 of a second.

▶ Athletes in action. By careful choice of camera lens and technique, the photographer can capture the spirit as well as the substance of the subject being photographed.

Photography is the science and art of permanently recording pictures of the world. A photograph can remind you of someone you love or bring back memories of things that are past. Photographs can be beautiful, impressive, informative, or funny. The complicated chemistry of photography has been mastered so completely that photographs can be taken, developed, and printed in less than a minute. Cameras have advanced so far that they can now operate completely automatically. Photography also allows us to look at things which we cannot see with our eyes alone because they move too quickly or too slowly, or are too far away. Photography is a means of mass communication also open to individuals.

14

Drawing with light

It is very simple to see an image of a brightly lit scene on a screen. The screen must be in a dark box with a small pinhole in the box, through which the light from the outside world can come to illuminate the screen. If the pinhole is the right size, there will be an image of the scene outside focused on the screen. This was known thousands of years ago. The device was called a camera obscura, which means "dark room." Although producing the image is simple, it is much more difficult to invent a screen which will permanently record the picture. This is the process of photography, which literally means "drawing with light."

The first-ever photograph was taken in the year 1826 by a French soldier called Joseph Nicéphore Niépce. He recorded the view from his window on a metal plate which had been coated with a light-sensitive substance. He had to wait all day for the picture to appear on the metal plate because the sensitivity of the coating on the plate was so low. Also, he did not use a lens to concentrate the light on the metal plate. Soon afterward he went into partnership with another Frenchman, who was called Louis Daguerre.

After Niépce's death, Daguerre invented a much more sensitive method of recording pictures, using copper plates coated with silver. The plates were first exposed to iodine fumes, which made the surface light-sensitive. The picture was taken, and then the plates were exposed to mercury vapor, which brought out the picture on the plate. The picture was fixed permanently by washing the plate in salty water.

Because the new coating was more sensitive to light, pictures could be taken more quickly. The reduced exposure times allowed photographs of people to be taken for the first time. The portraits were called daguerreotypes after their inventor and were very popular.

▲ This picture of a street in Paris was taken by Daguerre himself in 1833. It includes the first photographed human figure. Early photographs such as this one required very long exposure times. The man in the picture stood still to have his boots cleaned for a long enough time for his image to be recorded on the photographic plate.

► A new photographic technique was invented in 1851 which became more popular than the daguerreotype. It was called the wet-collodion process and involved coating a glass plate with a liquid and then exposing it to the light. Photographers had to carry chemicals with them and coat the plate inside the camera.

TENT PACKED FOR TRAVELLING

Negatives and positives

The first photographers were trying to find a way of recording a picture as a "positive" image. They wanted a process which would record the bright areas of the screen as white in the photograph and dark areas as black. (All early photographs were black and white.) This proved to be very difficult.

A breakthrough was made by an Englishman, William Fox Talbot. He found a relatively simple way of first producing a "negative" of the photograph, and then making a positive picture from the negative. His method of printing was very similar to that still used today, and allows many prints to be made from a single negative.

Modern photographic film consists of a thin layer, or emulsion, of a chemical called a silver halide on a transparent plastic sheet. The chemical is a combination of atoms of silver and atoms of one of the elements bromine, chlorine, iodine, or fluorine. These chemicals are sensitive to light. Normally transparent, they become black if they are exposed to light, or illuminated, so the film naturally records a negative picture in which the brightest areas of the scene produce the darkest area on the film.

A positive print can be made from the negative by placing the negative on a new piece of film and illuminating the film through the negative. This is called a contact print. The darkest areas of the negative produce the lightest areas on the print. If a print is required which is larger than the negative, the negative is held away from the film. Light shining through the negative then produces a larger image of it on the film.

▶ (top) A highly magnified view of a piece of unexposed photographic film, showing the crystals of silver halide. When light falls on the film, it produces some atoms of metallic silver within the crystals. (middle) Two crystals in which small areas have been blackened. If the exposed film were examined at this stage, there would be no picture to see. The film now has to be developed by immersing it in a chemical solution. In this solution the crystals blacken completely if they have been at all affected by light. (bottom) Crystals in the film after it has been developed. The picture is now visible on the film. The film is then immersed in a different solution, which washes away all the unblackened crystals of silver halide. The film is no longer sensitive to light, and the picture is permanently fixed on the film.

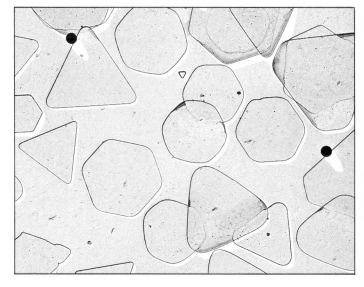

Color photography

Color photography also uses crystals of silver halide as the light-sensitive material in which to record a picture. Color film contains three layers of silver halide crystals. Each layer also contains chemicals which can form colored dyes. When the film is exposed to light, each layer reacts only to red, green, or blue light. After the film has been developed, each layer contains colored dye in the same places where the silver halide has been turned to silver. The dye colors are the complementary colors of those in the original image. For example, blue light results in yellow dye, and green light results in a magenta dye. The developed film therefore contains a color negative of the image.

▼ In color photography, the multilayered film is developed using a chemical which produces different colored dyes in the exposed parts of each layer. To print the image, white light is shined through the negative on paper having a similar multilayer coating. This reverses the colors, and the final print shows the same colors as the original image.

The color negative process

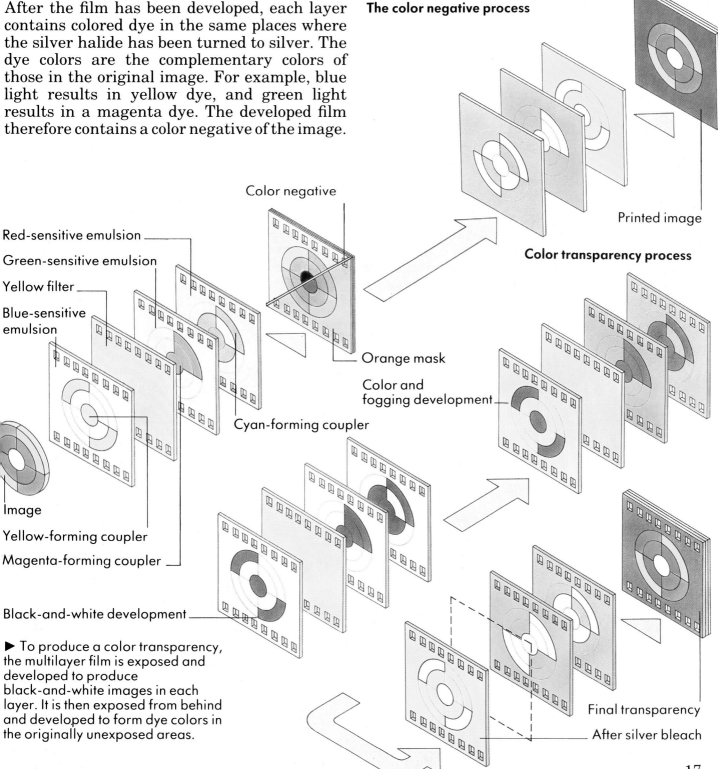

Color negative

Red-sensitive emulsion

Green-sensitive emulsion

Yellow filter

Blue-sensitive emulsion

Printed image

Color transparency process

Orange mask

Color and fogging development

Cyan-forming coupler

Image

Yellow-forming coupler

Magenta-forming coupler

Black-and-white development

Final transparency

After silver bleach

► To produce a color transparency, the multilayer film is exposed and developed to produce black-and-white images in each layer. It is then exposed from behind and developed to form dye colors in the originally unexposed areas.

Cameras

The first cameras were simple devices consisting of a box which held a single photographic plate, and a lens to focus light on the plate. Modern cameras can be extremely sophisticated electronic machines, with many functions automatically controlled. However, the principles of the camera are still the same. A roll of film loads into the back of the camera. Inside the camera it is completely dark until a picture is taken. A shutter inside the camera then opens to allow light coming through the lens to fall on the film. After a short time the shutter closes and the film can then be wound on to move an unexposed piece of film into position behind the shutter and lens. The main controls available are the lens position, the lens aperture size, and the exposure time.

Light from the scene to be photographed is focused on the film by the lens, or group of lenses, to produce a sharp image of the subject.

However, light coming from objects at different distances will focus at different positions behind the lens. To focus on subjects closer to the camera, the lens body is rotated, which screws it away from the camera body and the film. The aperture size is set by rotating a ring at the back of the lens.

Reducing the aperture will reduce the amount of light reaching the film. To compensate, the exposure time (the time for which the shutter is open) can be varied from a few seconds, for very dark scenes, to one-thousandth of a second. The very fast speed is used to photograph fast-moving objects so they do not appear blurred. Most cameras can automatically set the exposure time after the aperture size has been chosen. The amount of light in the scene is measured inside the camera, and the exposure time is set to allow the same amount of light to always hit the film.

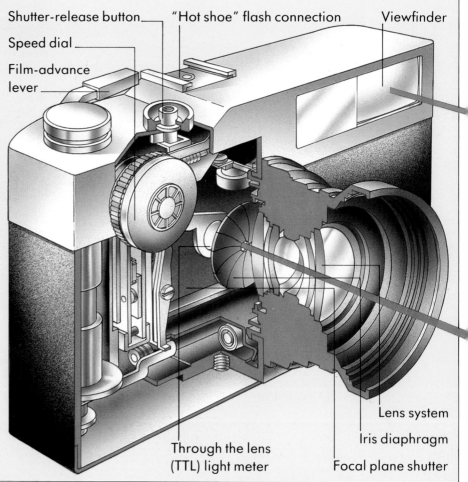

Pocket camera

The modern pocket camera is designed to be easy to use. The photographer composes a picture in the viewfinder and presses the shutter-release button. The shutter opens for a fraction of a second to expose one frame of the film, which captures an image of the scene viewed. Working the film-advance lever moves another frame of the film into position behind the shutter. The time of exposure is calculated automatically. A built-in light meter records the light level, and, acting on this information, the camera alters the shutter speed and/or lens aperture to give the correct exposure. The lens aperture is set by the iris diaphragm. This is made up of overlapping metal leaves, which advance or retract, depending on whether less or more light needs to enter. In low-level lighting conditions a flash is used to give adequate exposure. A flashgun is fixed into the "hot shoe," which has electrical contacts that cause the flash to be set off when the shutter opens.

Shutter-release button

Speed dial

Film-advance lever

"Hot shoe" flash connection

Viewfinder

Lens system

Iris diaphragm

Through the lens (TTL) light meter

Focal plane shutter

▶ This is an early camera, built in 1865, which used the collodion process. A plate of glass would be placed inside the back of the camera to record a single picture. The lens could be moved to focus the image. The chemicals needed to sensitize the glass were then put in the top of the camera. After the plate had been exposed to the image, further chemicals would be squeezed into the camera to process the photograph.

▼ The main type of camera in use today is the single lens reflex (SLR) camera. The SLR camera has only one lens (although this may consist of many optical components). The SLR camera can be fitted with many different types of lenses: zoom, telephoto, close-up, fisheye, which allow great variation in the focusing distance and in the angle of view of the camera. Many designs have automatic control of aperture size or shutter speed.

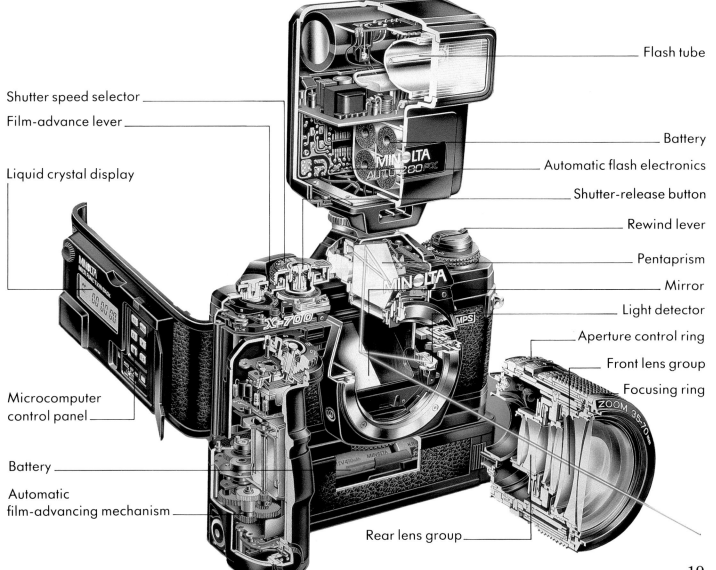

Flash tube

Shutter speed selector

Film-advance lever

Liquid crystal display

Battery

Automatic flash electronics

Shutter-release button

Rewind lever

Pentaprism

Mirror

Light detector

Aperture control ring

Front lens group

Focusing ring

Microcomputer control panel

Battery

Automatic film-advancing mechanism

Rear lens group

Advanced techniques

Photography was invented as a way of permanently recording scenes that people could see. Modern photography allows us to do much more than this. Pictures can be taken of things that we are unable to see. The normal human eye is sensitive to only a small range of the wavelengths of light. The shortest wavelength we can see is violet light; the longest is red light. Photographic film is not limited to this range. It can be designed to be sensitive to infrared wavelengths (longer than red) and ultraviolet wavelengths (shorter than violet). Some film can record wavelengths even shorter than ultraviolet, of which the most common to be used in photography are X-rays.

Photography also allows us to overcome other limiting features of the human eye. Some things happen too quickly to be seen, other things happen too slowly. High-speed photography and time-lapse photography make these events visible. High-speed photography involves taking a large number of pictures in a short time. It is important that in each picture the fast-moving object appear to be stationary so that the image is not blurred. This is achieved by using a flashing light as the illumination for the object. Each flash is a very short burst of bright light, which can repeat thousands of times a second.

Time-lapse photography involves taking frames of a film with long intervals between them. The film sequence is then played back at a much faster rate to speed up the apparent motion. This is a popular technique for showing such things as the growth of plants.

The human eye is also unable to see in very low levels of light. However, using photography, it is possible to build up a picture on sensitive film by collecting light over many hours. All the light hitting the film is recorded and contributes to the finished picture. This method is used in astronomical photography, for example in photographing dim and distant objects in the sky.

▼ A dragonfly in flight captured by high-speed photography. The exposure time is so short that the rapidly moving wings appear motionless.

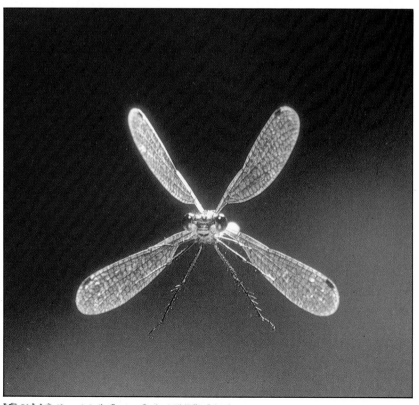

X-rays

X-rays are used to photograph internal regions of the body. X-rays are a form of electromagnetic radiation with a wavelength roughly one-thousandth that of visible light. The X-rays pass easily through soft tissue but are partly blocked by teeth and bones. Images of the teeth and bones show up on X-ray film placed behind a body.

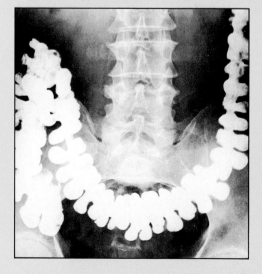

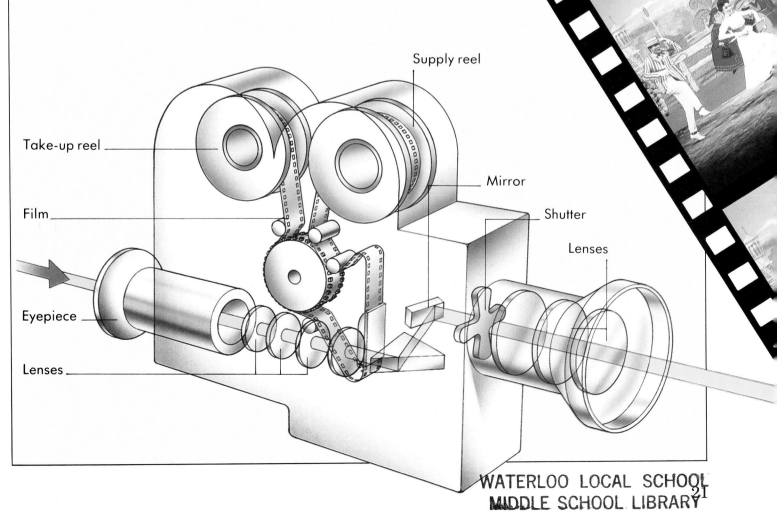

Moving-picture camera

A movie camera takes a large number of pictures on a long reel of film. When the film is played back at sufficient speed through a projector, the human brain does not see that each frame is separate. We receive an impression of smooth motion on the screen. To take the pictures, the film is fed into the camera by the rotation of the spools. The spools rotate continuously, but another mechanism stops the film behind the aperture for long enough for the exposure to be made. The film is then allowed to move on so that the next unexposed frame is brought into position. Most cameras take twenty-four frames every second, with each exposure time being one forty-eighth of a second. In the following forty-eighth of a second, the film has to be moved on and stopped again, ready for the next exposure.

Take-up reel

Film

Eyepiece

Lenses

Supply reel

Mirror

Shutter

Lenses

Telecommunications

Spot facts

• Transmission along the latest optical fibers can accommodate tens of thousands of telephone calls at a time.

• The craze for "videotex," or screen-based information systems, has been very successful in France. Over 10 million households have a miniature video terminal, or Minitel.

• Early Morse telegraph sets were able to transmit about 35 words per minute.

• The largest-ever private telegraph system was operated by the U.S. armed forces, with 2,700 centers in North and South America and 1,600 other centers around the world.

From a telephone in any house or office in a major city, a caller can dial a series of numbers and in a few seconds be connected to any telephone in one of a hundred different countries of the world. The telephone network provides a means of communication which is personal. Printing, television, radio, and recording are means of mass communication. The telephone system works through a vast network of cables which cross countries, continents, and oceans. Microwave stations beam our telephone calls through the air. Satellites are used to relay calls at the speed of light from one country to another. Telephone lines can also be used to carry digital information between computers.

▶ Talking on the telephone is the most personal form of telecommunication. Telephones can bring together in an instant people who may be thousands of kilometers apart at the opposite ends of the Earth.

22

Signals by wire

Electricity was first used in practical machines in the first half of the last century. One of the first useful applications of electricity was the construction of a device which could make the voltage at the end of a long wire the same as the voltage at the beginning. Normally, the voltage would decrease along the wire because of the electrical resistance of the wire. The new system worked by using the low-voltage strength remaining at the end of the cable to trigger an amplifying device. This boosted the signal back to its original strength to start the journey toward the next amplifying station. A scheme like this is necessary for all long-distance communication whether by wire or by optical fiber.

The first practical electrical communication machine used magnetic needles (like the needle of a compass) which were deflected in different directions, depending on the voltage signals it received along the wires from the sending machine. The same machine could both send and receive signals. The operator had to learn that each letter of the message was represented by a certain number of needle deflections.

The next advance was made by Samuel Morse and Alfred Vail, who installed the first of their communication systems in 1844. This used a code for each letter of the alphabet, consisting of a certain combination of dots and dashes. Common letters such as E and T were given short codes. Uncommon letters were given the long codes (for example T is "−" while V is "···−"). The operator sending the message would translate it into this Morse code during transmission and would tap out the code directly on an electrical contact of the sending device. The receiving device made a click for each tap of the contact. Two clicks close together indicated a dot; two further apart indicated a dash. Very high speeds could be achieved by skilled operators.

Many businesses have telex machines to provide a written record of telecommunications. A telex machine consists of a keyboard and printer, and often a display screen. The operator types the message and can check it on the screen. The message is transmitted as a series of on-off voltage pulses. The receiving machine decodes these and prints the message.

▼ An early design of Morse code receiver. The electrical signals arriving at the receiver would make a pen write dots or dashes on paper. Later designs simply made clicks for dots and dashes, and the receiving operator wrote the message out.

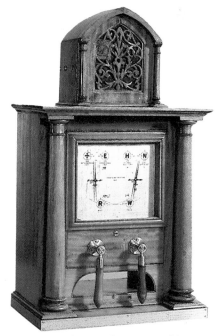

▲ A two-needle telegraph invented in England in 1837. This was an early practically instantaneous communication method between people who could not see each other. Experienced operators could read up to 20 words a minute.

The telephone

When you speak, you make sound waves in the air. The sound waves can be detected by the human ear so other people can hear what you are saying. The telephone is an instrument which can also respond to the sound waves of your voice and convert them into electrical signals. The signals travel along wires to the receiving telephone, where they are converted back into sound waves. These sound waves have to be similar to the original ones so that the person listening can understand what is being said.

The handset of a telephone consists of a microphone at one end and a loudspeaker at the other. When you speak into the microphone, the impact of the sound waves makes the surface vibrate. Behind the surface of the mouthpiece is a small chamber full of pieces of carbon. As the surface vibrates, the volume of the chamber changes and the carbon granules become more or less tightly packed. This changes the elect-rical resistance of the carbon. A current flows through one of the wires that come into the telephone. As the carbon resistance changes, the electric current in this wire also changes. It is this electric current which carries the record of the voice of the person using the phone. The changing electric current travels down wires and is routed by the local telephone central office to the right telephone.

When the current arrives at the receiving phone, it passes through coils wrapped around an electromagnet in the earpiece. The changing current produces in turn a changing magnetic field in the receiver. This either pulls or pushes a diaphragm, positioned behind the earpiece of the receiver. The vibrating surface reproduces the sound waves which were originally responsible for the varying current. Although the reproduction is not perfect, somebody listening can usually understand what was said into the calling telephone.

▲ Early telephone systems were run by operators connecting calls by hand. This was a slow process, and prone to mistakes.

▶ Modern telephone systems are all electronic. Connections to the dialed telephone number are made automatically. Human intervention is needed only for maintenance.

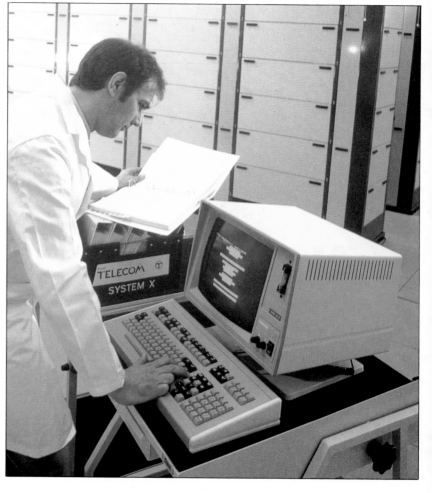

Telephone network

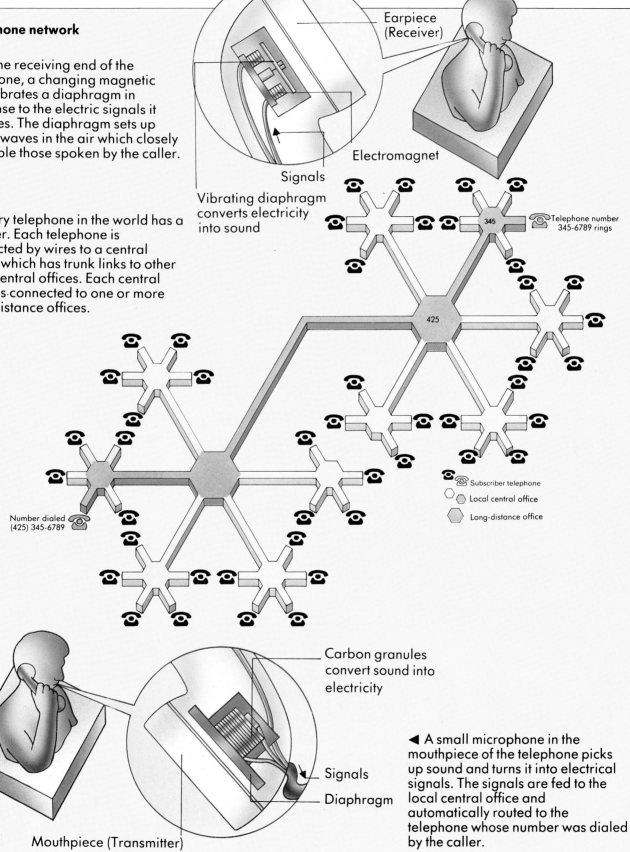

▶ At the receiving end of the telephone, a changing magnetic field vibrates a diaphragm in response to the electric signals it receives. The diaphragm sets up sound waves in the air which closely resemble those spoken by the caller.

▶ Every telephone in the world has a number. Each telephone is connected by wires to a central office, which has trunk links to other local central offices. Each central office is connected to one or more long-distance offices.

Earpiece (Receiver)

Electromagnet

Signals

Vibrating diaphragm converts electricity into sound

Telephone number 345-6789 rings

Subscriber telephone

Local central office

Long-distance office

Number dialed (425) 345-6789

Carbon granules convert sound into electricity

Signals

Diaphragm

◀ A small microphone in the mouthpiece of the telephone picks up sound and turns it into electrical signals. The signals are fed to the local central office and automatically routed to the telephone whose number was dialed by the caller.

Mouthpiece (Transmitter)

Cable links

Individual telephones are connected to a local central office. The network linking local central offices throughout the country is made up of trunk lines. These may use fiber optics or microwave transmissions or may rely on coaxial cable.

Coaxial cable consists of a central conductor surrounded by an electrically insulating plastic which is itself surrounded by a conducting cylinder.

Multiplexing

Because of the expense of laying cables and the increasing demand for telephone lines, it has been important to develop ways of using a single cable for many telephone calls at a time. This is called multiplexing. A common system of multiplexing involves pulse code modulation (PCM). Instead of sending the complete telephone signal along the cable, the strength of the signal is measured eight thousand times a second. This is called digitizing the signal. Each value of signal strength is represented as an eight-digit binary number consisting of ones and zeros. These numbers are sent along the cable, and the original signal is reconstructed at the receiver. Because the binary number can be transmitted very rapidly, the cable is used for only a very short period every one eight-thousandth of a second to transmit information for one telephone call. It is possible to send many other calls at the same time along the same cable by interleaving signal strength information from other telephones.

▼ A chaotic mass of telephone cables in Kansas, in 1909. When telephones were first invented, every telephone had to be connected to every other telephone by two wires. Even after the installation of local central offices, every simultaneous call into the office had to arrive by a different wire. The solution to this problem arrived with the invention of multiplexing.

There are cables which carry telephone calls across seas and oceans. The cables lie on the seabed and have to be strong enough to withstand the huge pressure of water pressing down upon them. The first cable across the Atlantic Ocean was laid in 1956 and could originally carry up to 36 simultaneous telephone calls. There are now a number of cables between Europe and the American continent. The recent transatlantic telephone cable called TAT-8 was the first optical-fiber link. It can carry nearly 40,000 telephone calls at the same time.

▶ A telecommunications cable made up of optical fibers: thin, flexible glass threads. Optical-fiber cables are now laid by telecommunications companies in preference to copper ones. They have many times the capacity of copper cables, being able to carry tens of thousands of telephone calls at once. The glass used for making optical fibers is so pure that a block 20 km (12 mi.) thick would be transparent.

Optical-fiber transmission

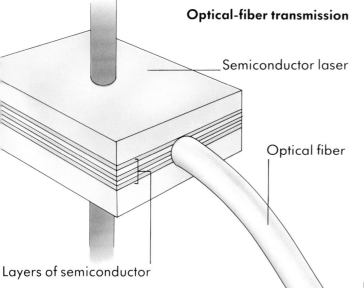

Semiconductor laser

Optical fiber

Layers of semiconductor

▲ Optical fibers are made from pure quartz glass. This material can be drawn out into very long strands with a small diameter. The fiber is surrounded by a cladding and also a plastic sheath. Pulses of light are sent into the fiber by laser, and travel through it by bouncing off the inside wall of the fiber. The design of the fiber ensures that no light escapes through the side wall. The first optical-fiber transatlantic telephone cable (photo), TAT-8, went into service in 1988.

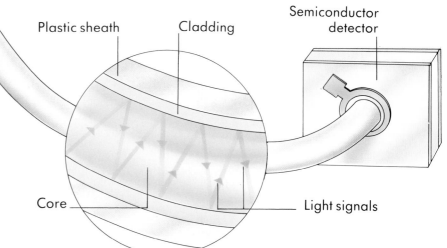

Plastic sheath   Cladding

Semiconductor detector

Core

Light signals

Microwave links

Microwaves are a form of radiation with a wavelength longer than visible light but shorter than radio waves. The wavelengths used in communications are often between 5 cm (2 in.) and 10 cm (4 in.). The minimum range for a telephone channel is about 3 kHz (3,000 Hz, or cycles per second). Any region of the frequency spectrum which is 3 kHz wide can be used to transmit a telephone call. A carrier frequency can be added to the spoken frequencies before transmission, and then subtracted after reception to return the range to audible sound. All communications systems have a range of frequencies which they can transmit. Splitting this "bandwidth" into different channels is called frequency division multiplexing. Microwaves used in communications typically have a frequency of 3-6 million kHz (3-6 GHz), and so thousands of phone calls can occupy a bandwidth only a small fraction of this.

Microwaves are used to transmit telephone calls through the air. They can be focused to a beam and sent between transmitters and receivers over 50 km (30 mi.) apart. They are also used in satellite communications. The signals are sent up with a bandwidth centred around a frequency of, say, 4 GHz, and returned around a central frequency of 6 GHz.

Most communications satellites are geo-stationary. They orbit the Earth at a height of nearly 36,000 km (over 22,000 mi.), always remaining above the same point.

▲ A microwave relay tower in Florida. Beams of microwaves carrying telephone calls are captured in the detectors, called horns, which are mounted on top of the tower. The signals can then be amplified and redirected to other receiving towers or passed into the cable telephone system.

► Very-high-frequency (VHF) waves are sent in straight lines between tall towers, or bounced off orbiting satellites. Shortwaves can be made to bounce back to Earth from the ionosphere.

Long-distance radio transmission

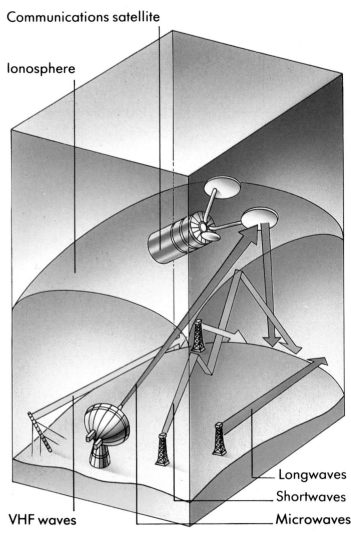

Communications satellite

Ionosphere

Longwaves

Shortwaves

Microwaves

VHF waves

Fax and electronic mail

Both facsimile (known as fax) and electronic mail (e-mail) are ways of sending documents without using the conventional mailing system. Both are much faster than ordinary mail, and both make use of telephone lines to transmit information. Fax and e-mail use a device called a modem (short for modulator-demodulator). The modem converts digital information from a fax machine or a computer into a sound signal which can be sent along a telephone line. A modem at the other end of the line changes this signal back to the original format.

The fax machine can transmit any document, whether it contains words or pictures. The document is placed in the machine, which then pulls it over a strip of bright light. A scanner measures the reflectivity of the paper. White areas reflect the light much more than areas with writing or drawing on them. This information is recorded in a sequence of numbers. For each small area of paper, a one or a zero is added to the sequence depending on whether the page is light or dark at that point. This information is then sent along a telephone line to the receiving fax machine, where it is used to make a copy of the original page.

E-mail provides a way for people with computers to communicate with each other. A computer can be linked to the telephone system using a modem. The sender types out the message and instructs the computer to send it. The information is converted into a signal for transmission along a telephone line. At the destination computer, the signal may be reconverted and shown on the receiver's screen at once. Or if that computer is switched off or in use, the message can be stored in the central memory bank for later retrieval. By this method messages can be transmitted purely as electronic signals, without ever being printed.

Facsimile (fax) system

The scanner reads the information of light and dark on the document. The information is coded into binary digits, then converted by a modem into a telephone signal. Transmitted via a relay tower, the signal is reconverted to a binary sequence at the receiving end.

The receiving fax machine then creates a duplicate of the original document by exposing light-sensitive paper to bright illumination on those areas which were white in the original document. International fax messages may be transmitted by satellite.

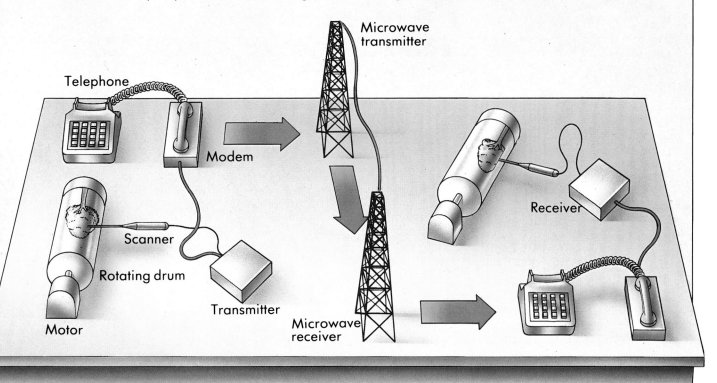

On the air

- The first use of the radiomicrophone was in 1947. Reg Moores, an entertainer, used it in an ice-spectacular in Brighton, England.

- 30 images, or 6,000 billion billion electrons, are normally transmitted by television every second. Images persist in the human eye for one-tenth of a second, so television must produce more than ten images per second to give the impression of a moving image.

- In the United States, any one television station uses as much space on the airwaves as all the AM radio stations put together.

- The first videophones appeared in the early 1970s. As the speaker's voice was relayed by telephone, his or her image was transmitted on a screen by closed-circuit television.

▶ The scene in a television broadcasting studio during the screening of the news and weather. A number of cameras view the anchorpersons, who read from notes and TelePrompTer screens.

Television and radio are the most used forms of mass communication. They are also the main source of entertainment in the home. Television and radio are broadcast from transmitters, which send their signals through the air in all directions. The signals can be picked up by an antenna connected to an individual set.

The advent of television has changed the view we have of the world, making it seem smaller. Live television broadcasts allow us to see events as they happen. We can watch momentous world events from the other side of the planet. We can have the best view in the sports stadium, and hear commentary on the game at the same time. Satellites which orbit the Earth at a height of nearly 36,000 km (over 22,000 mi.) are used to relay television signals from distant places into our homes.

Wireless telegraph

About one hundred years ago it was discovered that electric and magnetic energy could travel through the air, or even through empty space. This is called electromagnetic radiation. It was calculated that the speed at which this radiation should move was the same as the speed of light. It was realized that visible light is a kind of electromagnetic radiation, but that there are very many other kinds of electromagnetic radiation which are invisible to humans. These include what we now call gamma rays, X-rays, ultraviolet and infrared radiation, microwaves, and radio waves.

In all early forms of electrical communication, information was carried by an electric current traveling along a wire. Following the discovery of electromagnetic radiation, some people saw the possibility of using it to create a form of communication without wires. This wireless telegraph was developed in particular by an Italian called Guglielmo Marconi. His first working system used electric sparks to generate the electromagnetic radiation, and a coil of wire which could be attached to an earpiece to detect the radiation. The radio waves radiated from the spark in all directions. Some passed through the coil, which generated a current in the loop of wire. This was used to create a faint clicking sound in the earpiece.

Using this system, Marconi could send messages in Morse code between people who were not connected by a wire. In 1896 he sent Morse code messages for a short distance between a spark generator and a receiver. In 1901 he sent messages over 3,000 km (nearly 2,000 mi.) across the Atlantic Ocean. It surprised everybody that the radio waves could be received from so far away. In fact, radio waves are reflected by the ionosphere and reach the Earth many thousands of kilometers away.

Electromagnetic waves

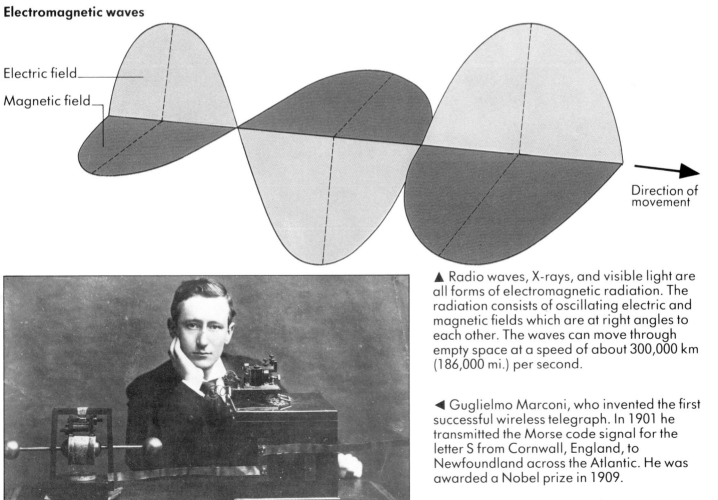

Electric field

Magnetic field

Direction of movement

▲ Radio waves, X-rays, and visible light are all forms of electromagnetic radiation. The radiation consists of oscillating electric and magnetic fields which are at right angles to each other. The waves can move through empty space at a speed of about 300,000 km (186,000 mi.) per second.

◄ Guglielmo Marconi, who invented the first successful wireless telegraph. In 1901 he transmitted the Morse code signal for the letter S from Cornwall, England, to Newfoundland across the Atlantic. He was awarded a Nobel prize in 1909.

Radio

Radio waves are a type of electromagnetic radiation. All electromagnetic radiation has a wavelength and a frequency. The wavelength is the distance between the peaks of the wave. The frequency is the number of times the wave goes up and down in a second. Wavelength is measured in meters; frequency is measured in hertz (Hz), kilohertz (kHz), or megahertz (MHz). A megahertz is a thousand kilohertz.

The first transatlantic radio messages of Marconi consisted of radiation over a range of frequencies which were sent in three short bursts to spell out the letter S in Morse code. With improvements in electronics at the beginning of the century, it became possible to produce radio waves at almost a single frequency. Radio receivers were also invented which could be tuned to detect a signal at a single frequency.

These two developments allow many radio stations to broadcast each on a different frequency for the listener to choose from. Radio broadcasts in the United States are made in two ranges of frequencies. "AM" broadcasts have a frequency between 535 and 1,605 kHz. The band called FM is between 88 and 108 MHz.

A radio system consists of a microphone linked to a transmitter, and a receiver linked to a loudspeaker. When someone speaks or plays music into the microphone, the sound waves are converted into electrical signals. These signals are then mixed with a radio wave. This is called modulation. The radio wave is called the carrier wave.

The radio wave with all the sound information on it is then beamed in all directions from high-power transmitters. A radio antenna can detect these radio waves passing across it. The antenna detects all frequencies, but by tuning the radio to a particular position only one frequency is amplified within the radio. The radio subtracts the carrier wave from the signal, which leaves the original sound information. This is used to drive a loudspeaker, which makes the sound from the radio audible.

▼ Radio signals controlling model aircraft. The joystick controls produce different signals depending on the direction of movement. The large antenna sends out the signal, which is picked up by a receiver on the plane. This controls the wings and rudder.

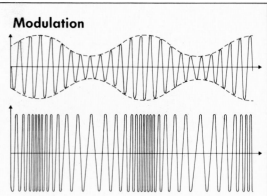

Modulation

Modulation is the process of adding information to a radio wave. A pure radio wave has a constant frequency and a constant signal strength (amplitude). It is possible either to change the amplitude of the carrier wave or to change its frequency to make it carry sound information to a radio receiver. These two methods are called amplitude modulation (AM) and frequency modulation (FM).

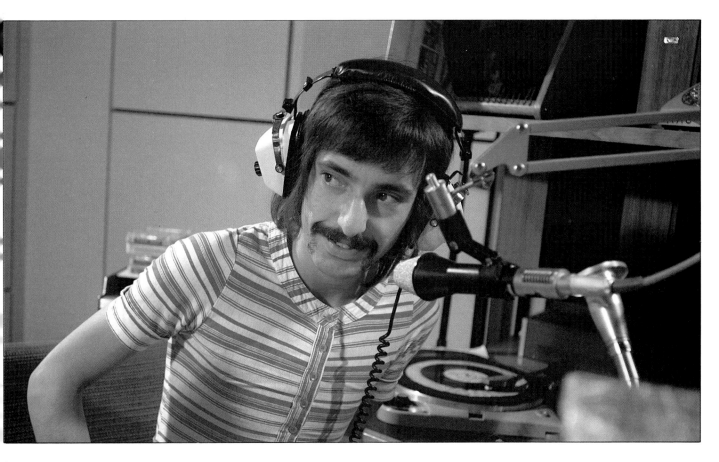

Cellular telephone

▲ An FM radio DJ (disk jockey) speaks to a caller on a popular "phone-in" program. FM radio stations broadcast from transmitters which have only a limited, above-the-horizon range.

▲ Using a portable cellular telephone, a cross between a telephone handset and a "walkie-talkie" radio.

▶ In a cellular telephone system, telephones link into the telephone network via local transmitters.

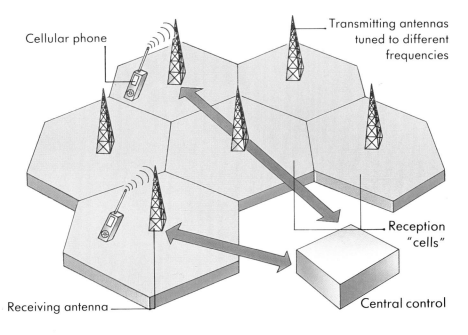

Cellular phone

Transmitting antennas tuned to different frequencies

Reception "cells"

Receiving antenna

Central control

Television

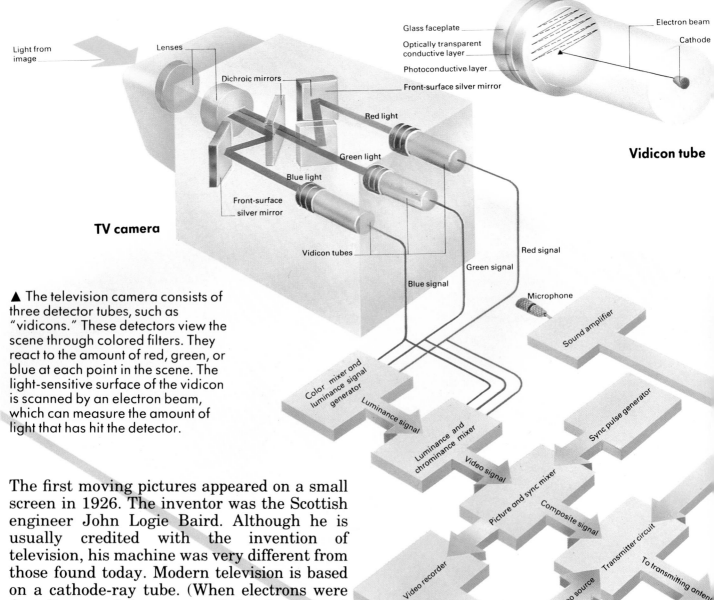

Light from image

Lenses

Dichroic mirrors

Front-surface silver mirror

Red light

Green light

Blue light

Front-surface silver mirror

TV camera

Vidicon tubes

Glass faceplate

Optically transparent conductive layer

Photoconductive layer

Electron beam

Cathode

Vidicon tube

Red signal

Green signal

Blue signal

Microphone

Sound amplifier

Color mixer and luminance signal generator

Luminance signal

Luminance and chrominance mixer

Video signal

Sync pulse generator

Picture and sync mixer

Composite signal

Video recorder

Alternative video source

Transmitter circuit

To transmitting antenna

▲ The television camera consists of three detector tubes, such as "vidicons." These detectors view the scene through colored filters. They react to the amount of red, green, or blue at each point in the scene. The light-sensitive surface of the vidicon is scanned by an electron beam, which can measure the amount of light that has hit the detector.

The first moving pictures appeared on a small screen in 1926. The inventor was the Scottish engineer John Logie Baird. Although he is usually credited with the invention of television, his machine was very different from those found today. Modern television is based on a cathode-ray tube. (When electrons were first discovered they were called cathode rays.) The front of the tube forms the screen of the television. Behind the screen of a color television there are three electron guns which use a high voltage to speed up electrons and accelerate them toward the screen.

When electrons hit a point on the screen, they make that position glow with a colour which depends on a chemical with which the screen is coated. A color television screen is coated with three different chemicals (called phosphors) which glow red, green, or blue. The picture is built up from dots or lines of only these colors. From a normal viewing distance these primary colors merge to reproduce the color in the scene being televised. From close to the screen,

▲ The three color signals from the vidicon light detectors in the television camera are combined to form a chrominance signal, which measures the amount of each color. The three signals are also used to measure the overall brightness of each part of the scene. This is the luminance signal. The chrominance and luminance signals are combined with the sound signal before being transmitted from the antenna.

the individual areas of primary colour are easily visible.

The screen is divided into many hundreds of horizontal lines of phosphors: 625 lines in parts of Europe, 525 in the United States and Japan. The electron beams are scanned across the screen, illuminating only a single point on the screen at any instant. The electrons are deflected by magnets, which scan the beam from left to right across the first line. The beam then jumps back across the screen and scans the third line, also from left to right. The scanning continues on every other line until the bottom of the screen is reached. This takes one-sixtieth of a second. The beam then jumps back to the second line and fills in the even-numbered lines in the same way. A complete screen is drawn in one-thirtieth of a second. This scanning rate of thirty frames a second is enough for the scanning to be invisible to the human eye.

▼ The signal is picked up by the antenna. It is passed into the TV set, where it is split into its constituent parts. The sound signal goes to the loudspeaker. The luminance and chrominance information goes to the electron guns, which illuminate the phosphors on the screen so as to produce a color image of the scene as viewed by the camera.

▼ The three electron beams are fired toward the screen. The screen is coated with lines of blue, green, and red phosphors which glow with color when they are energized by the electrons.

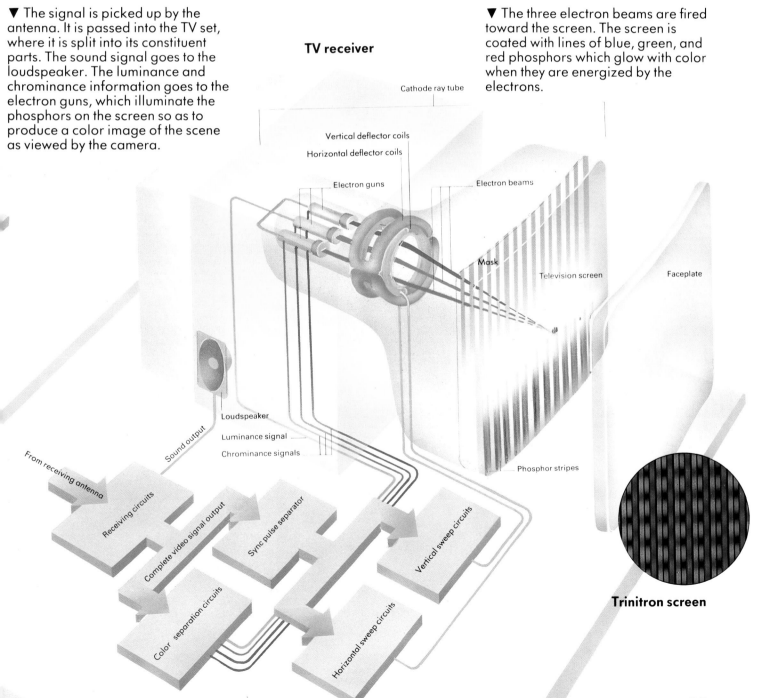

TV receiver

Cathode ray tube

Vertical deflector coils

Horizontal deflector coils

Electron guns

Electron beams

Mask

Television screen

Faceplate

Loudspeaker

Luminance signal

Chrominance signals

From receiving antenna

Sound output

Receiving circuits

Complete video signal output

Sync pulse separator

Vertical sweep circuits

Color separation circuits

Horizontal sweep circuits

Phosphor stripes

Trinitron screen

On screen

Television is an extremely popular source of entertainment and information. In Western Europe there is a television in most homes. In the United States there are almost as many televisions as there are people in the country. The widespread ownership of television sets and the enthusiasm of people for watching them make broadcasting on television a very efficient way of reaching the attention of millions of viewers. Companies pay large amounts of money to advertise their products in breaks during and between programs.

In most countries the broadcasting organizations are separate from the government, and many are independent companies. By transmitting their programs on cable networks or via satellite, they provide many different channels.

A television antenna will pick up programs sent through the air from powerful transmitting towers. Television programs can also arrive in the home along cables or from a satellite. In a cable TV network, a wire runs from each house to a main cable. The main cable is connected to either a local receiving antenna or directly to the television station. Cable TV has become widespread in cities in the United States, where the many tall steel buildings make conventional TV reception difficult.

Television signals can also be transmitted from the TV station to one of the communications satellites that orbit the Earth. The satellite receives the transmissions and sends them back to Earth, radiating the signal over a large area of land. The programs are picked up by means of a small dish antenna.

In addition to broadcasting programs, television can display pages of information. The information may be sent by the TV company, with the TV owner having to install an electronic unit which decodes the signal and displays the text. A similar system called viewdata allows access to banks of information via a telephone line. The databank can be questioned and the answer shown on the screen.

Cable television

People who subscribe to a cable-TV network watch television programs received not via an external antenna, but via cable. The network control station (picture right) receives programs beamed down to it from one or more communications satellites.

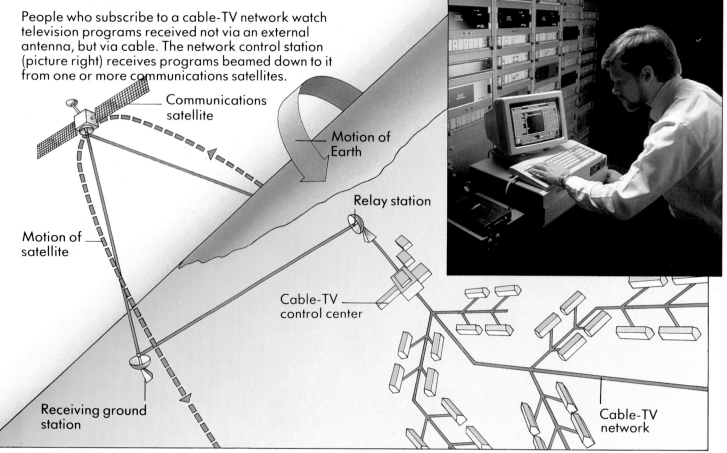

Communications satellite

Motion of Earth

Motion of satellite

Relay station

Cable-TV control center

Receiving ground station

Cable-TV network

▲ A watch TV, which uses a liquid crystal display (LCD) to create a black-and-white picture. The screen is made up of liquid-crystal cells, which change their reflectivity when an electric field is applied to them. Other new technologies are leading to the development of full-size flat-screen TV receivers.

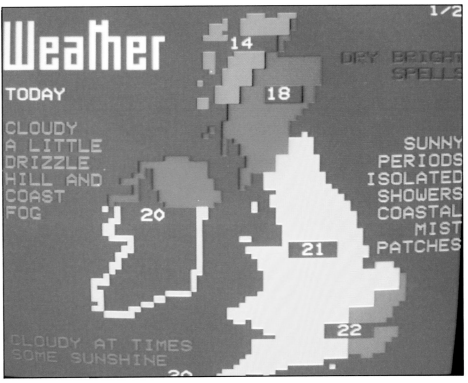

▲ The weather "page" of the Ceefax information "magazine" broadcast on television by the British Broadcasting Corporation (BBC). The BBC pioneered the system, called teletext, in the 1970s.

▼ Closed-circuit television being used at the Live Aid pop concert in London in 1985 to give the audience a better view of the performers. The concert was also relayed worldwide by satellite.

Recording

▶ Young people gyrate to the throbbing music at a discotheque in Disneyland, near Los Angeles, USA. Disco dancing to records remains as popular as ever. But for personal listening, cassette tapes or compact disks are now preferred.

Sound can be recorded and replayed in many different ways. The methods which are in everyday use are magnetic tape, the record, and the compact disk. To record on tape, the sound is converted to electric signals, which are used to alter the magnetism of the tape. To manufacture a record, the sound vibrations are fed to a cutter, which makes a wavy groove in a "master" disk. For the compact disk the sound is converted to a string of numbers, which represent the sound waves. The numbers are recorded on the disk and "read" by laser.

The more difficult problem of recording picture information can also be solved using either magnetic tape (video) or laser-read disks. The main use of these inventions is in home entertainment and in broadcasting.

Microphones and speakers

Sound waves are a variation in air pressure. Microphones have to use this varying air pressure to produce a similar variation in a voltage or current within the microphone. In that way, electrical signals can be sent along wires from the microphone. Two major types of microphone in use today are the dynamic microphone and the condenser microphone. Both types have a thin sheet, or diaphragm, behind a protective front cover.

In the dynamic microphone, there is a coil of wire attached behind the diaphragm. A movement of the diaphragm in response to the varying air pressure of sound waves moves the coil past a magnet in the microphone. This creates a varying electric current in the coil. In the condenser microphone, the diaphragm movement changes the spacing between it and a second sheet or plate positioned behind it. This changes an electrical property called capacitance. As the capacitance changes, electric current travels along the wires from the microphone.

Loudspeakers

Loudspeakers have to convert a varying electrical signal into sound. The common dynamic loudspeaker does this by using the signal to move the thin cone which forms the front of the speaker. The movement sets up air pressure variations, which reproduce the original sound. The speaker operates in a similar way to the dynamic microphone. A coil of wire, which is attached to the speaker cone, sits in the field of a magnet. The electric signal is fed into the coil, which causes it to move in the magnetic field. This makes the speaker cone vibrate to match the oscillations of the electric current.

To reproduce accurately the original sounds, it is important to have a range of speakers of different physical size. Small speakers (called tweeters) are good for reproducing high-pitched sounds. Large speakers (called woofers) are best for low-pitched sounds. The accuracy of sound reproduction is called fidelity. Some very high fidelity (hi-fi) speakers have three cones, each for a different frequency range.

▼ Microphones convert the pressure variations of sound waves into similar variations in electric current. In a condenser microphone the movement of the diaphragm changes the distance between it and a charged plate. This changes the amount of charge the plate can hold. As it changes, current is moved along the wires from the microphone.

Microphone

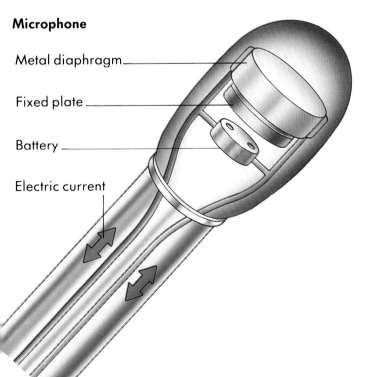

Metal diaphragm

Fixed plate

Battery

Electric current

Loudspeaker

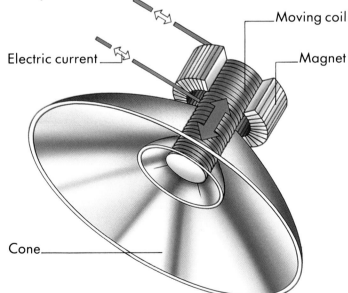

Electric current

Moving coil

Magnet

Cone

▲ When the varying electric current reaches a dynamic loudspeaker, it is fed to a coil. The coil sits in a magnetic field. Changes in the current alter the amount of force which the magnetic field exerts on the coil. The coil moves backward and forward inside the magnet. The coil is attached to a thin cone. The cone moves the air around it to reproduce the pressure variations in the original sounds.

Record and tape

Sound can be permanently recorded and played back using magnetic tape (reel-to-reel and cassette) or plastic phonograph records. To record on a magnetic tape, the electric signal from a microphone is fed to an electromagnet which forms the main part of the recording head of a tape recorder. The tape is drawn past the recording head as it is wound from one spool to the other. It is very important that this movement be smooth. When the tape is played back, it has to move at the same speed as that of the recording. The tape has a thin layer of tiny metallic crystals of iron oxide. Each one of the crystals can act as a magnet. When the tape passes over the recording head, the crystals are magnetized so that the poles point in a particular direction. When the tape is played back, the process is reversed. The magnetization of the crystals induces currents in the replay head, which are passed to a loudspeaker to reproduce the original sounds.

Recording on magnetic tape is also the first step in making a phonograph record. The taped sounds are fed to a cutter, which scores a groove in a "lacquer"-coated aluminum disk. The waviness of the groove contains the information about the volume and pitch of the original sounds. This first disk is then used to produce a metal copy. The metal copy has ridges which

▼ A recent very successful development in tape technology is the personal stereo, often called a walkman. Great effort was invested by many Japanese companies, particularly Sony, in the miniaturization of the tape player and in the design and appearance of the product.

The pioneers

Toward the end of the 1800s two systems of sound reproduction were invented. The reel-to-reel system, invented by the Dane Valdemar Poulsen, stored sound on a magnetized steel wire. The wax cylinder system was invented by Thomas Edison (right). It stored sound in grooves in the wax.

exactly match the grooves in the original disk. Two metal copies are required, one for each side of the record. To produce a record, blank plastic disks are pressed between the two metal masters. This produces a groove in each side of the disk, which is a copy of the original. When the stylus of the record player runs in the groove, its vibrations are picked up and translated into electrical signals. The signals are amplified and fed to the speakers of the system.

To make a stereo recording on a disk, the groove is produced by two cutters. Each cutter forms the shape of one side of the valley of the groove. When the record is played, the effect on the stylus from the two differently shaped sides of the groove can be split up in the stylus cartridge. Two signals are sent from the pickup arm to the amplifier. The amplified signals are then sent to separate loudspeakers, which together reproduce stereophonic sounds.

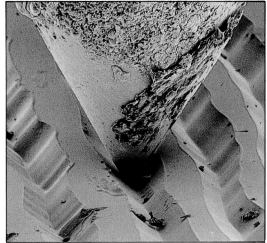

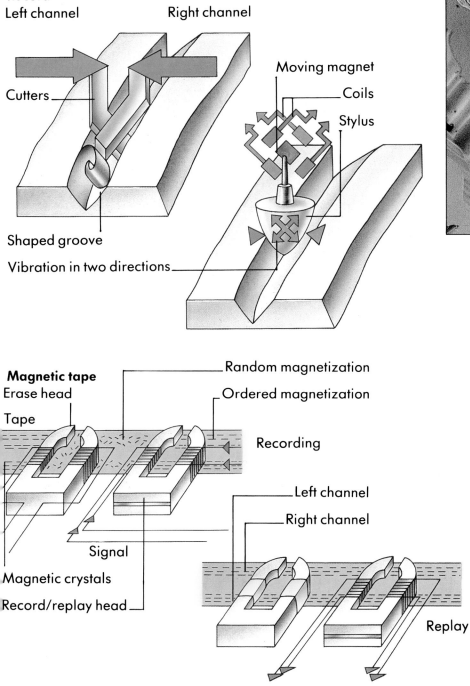

Record

Left channel — Right channel

Cutters

Shaped groove

Vibration in two directions

Moving magnet — Coils

Stylus

Magnetic tape

Erase head

Tape

Random magnetization

Ordered magnetization

Recording

Left channel

Right channel

Signal

Magnetic crystals

Record/replay head

Replay

◄▲ Sound is stored on plastic records in the shape of the groove which is cut in the disk. The original sound is fed to cutters, which shape a long spiral groove in a lacquer-coated disk. Stereo sound is reproduced by cutting the two sides of the groove with different shapes. The sound is reproduced by a diamond stylus (photo above) which runs in the groove and vibrates as it is moved by the wavy edges. Sound is stored on tape in the magnetism of a thin layer of iron oxide crystals which coat the plastic tape. Varying currents from a microphone change the strength of the magnetic field of the recording head. This magnetizes the crystals in particular directions. Running the tape past the replay head induces electric currents, which are fed to a loudspeaker. Stereo recordings can also be made on magnetic tape. The recording is made in two tracks at different positions across the tape. The sounds on each track are played back through loudspeakers.

41

Video

Television pictures can be stored on videotape in the same way that sound can be recorded on audiotape. The two kinds of tape are made from similar materials: magnetized iron oxide particles on a plastic tape. But vastly more information has to be put on the videotape than on the audio cassette. Thirty times every second the video recording head has to put information on the tape. This information is on the brightness and color at each point of the 525 lines of the television screen.

The first video machines which used magnetic tape tried to use exactly the same recording technique as an audio tape recorder. The recording head was kept stationary and the tape was moved past it. Because of the enormous amount of information that had to be recorded, the tape had to be moved extremely quickly over the head. Speeds of up to ten meters (over 30 ft.) per second were used. Modern video recorders move the tape at only two centimeters (less than 1 in.) per second, five hundred times slower. The decrease in speed has been made possible by improvements in the way that television picture information is put on tape by the recording head.

Modern video recorders

Instead of moving the tape very quickly past the head, modern video recorders move the head very quickly past the tape by putting it on a cylinder which is rotated at high speed. When a videotape is put into a videocassette recorder (VCR), the cover that protects the tape is lifted and two plastic posts rise behind the tape and pull it out of the cassette. The tape is wrapped around the recording head cylinder. The cylinder contains two recording/play heads which rotate with it. The cylinder is twice as wide as the tape and set at an angle to it. As the cylinder rotates beneath the angled tape, the recording heads write the information on the tape in long diagonal lines, which run from one edge of the tape to the other.

There are two main VCR systems: Betamax and VHS (Video Home System). Both use tape that is 12.7 mm (0.5 in.) wide.

▼ The use of a video camera recorder (camcorder) for recording family events and holidays is becoming more and more popular. Simple camcorders are available now which record picture and sound at the same time. Tapes recorded like this can be played back on standard VCR machines.

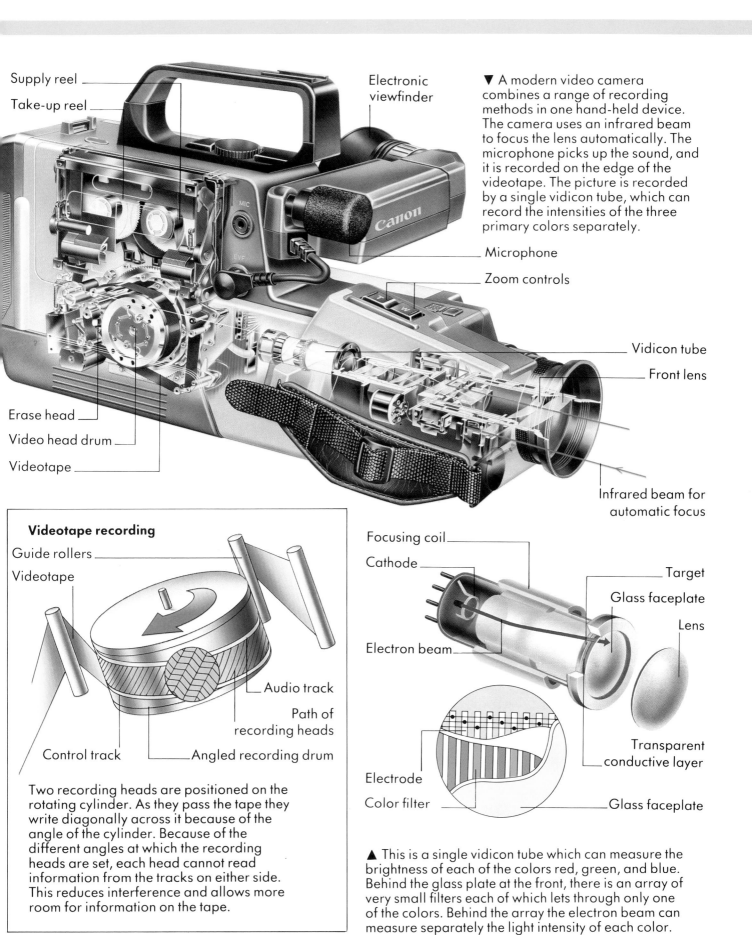

Supply reel

Take-up reel

Electronic viewfinder

▼ A modern video camera combines a range of recording methods in one hand-held device. The camera uses an infrared beam to focus the lens automatically. The microphone picks up the sound, and it is recorded on the edge of the videotape. The picture is recorded by a single vidicon tube, which can record the intensities of the three primary colors separately.

Microphone

Zoom controls

Vidicon tube

Front lens

Erase head

Video head drum

Videotape

Infrared beam for automatic focus

Videotape recording

Guide rollers

Videotape

Audio track

Path of recording heads

Control track

Angled recording drum

Two recording heads are positioned on the rotating cylinder. As they pass the tape they write diagonally across it because of the angle of the cylinder. Because of the different angles at which the recording heads are set, each head cannot read information from the tracks on either side. This reduces interference and allows more room for information on the tape.

Focusing coil

Cathode

Target

Glass faceplate

Lens

Electron beam

Electrode

Color filter

Transparent conductive layer

Glass faceplate

▲ This is a single vidicon tube which can measure the brightness of each of the colors red, green, and blue. Behind the glass plate at the front, there is an array of very small filters each of which lets through only one of the colors. Behind the array the electron beam can measure separately the light intensity of each color.

Digital disks

A relatively new form of recording to reach the home is the compact disk. The disks themselves and the disk players require very precise and controlled manufacturing methods. This makes them probably the most complicated and advanced machines that are in everyday use in the home.

There are three main features of compact disks which make the quality of the sound obtainable from them superior. The first is that sound is recorded digitally on them, and played back digitally. The second is that unlike the stylus of a record player, or the recording head of a tape recorder, the device used to "read" the sound does not actually touch the disk. This removes the danger of damage to the disk and even prevents the usual wear and tear. The third is that special circuitry corrects errors on the disk. These features combine to improve the sound quality and the lifetime of the disk.

▼ A compact disk is 120 mm (4.7 in.) in diameter and 1.2 mm (0.047 in.) thick. It can store up to 74 minutes of music. A close-up of the surface of the disk (right) shows the pattern of pits which store the sounds.

In digital recording, the sound is not recorded as the depth of a groove nor the magnetization patterns on a tape. Its intensity is converted into a binary number, and this number is put on the disk. All the zeros in the number are represented by small pits in the disk.

Reading by laser

As a laser scans the disk, its light is reflected efficiently by the smooth surface of the disk but is scattered in all directions when it strikes a pit in the surface. By measuring changes in the brightness of the reflected light, the disk player can read the lines of zeros or ones that represent the sound intensity values. By converting these intensities to electrical signals which drive a loudspeaker, the original sound is read from the disk and reproduced so that it can be heard.

The laser beam is scanned in a spiral beneath the disk by a system of mirrors and lenses. The beam is focused on the recorded surface through the plastic cover of the disk. Lasers are used because they are very bright and can be focused on very small spots.

To reduce the likelihood of making a mistake in reading the disk, information about the sound values is recorded in more than one place on the disk. Special error-detection codes are included in the information. If the compact disk player detects an error, perhaps because of a scratch or mistake in manufacture, it will probably be able to correct it.

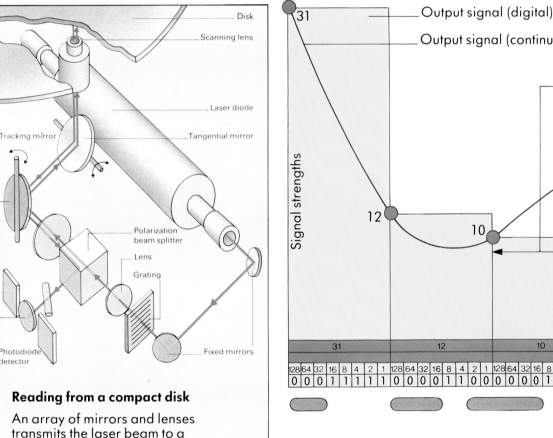

Reading from a compact disk

An array of mirrors and lenses transmits the laser beam to a scanning lens which focuses the laser light on the underside of the disk. As the disk rotates, the lens follows the spiral track of sound information. The mirrors also move to keep the beam pointed at the lens.

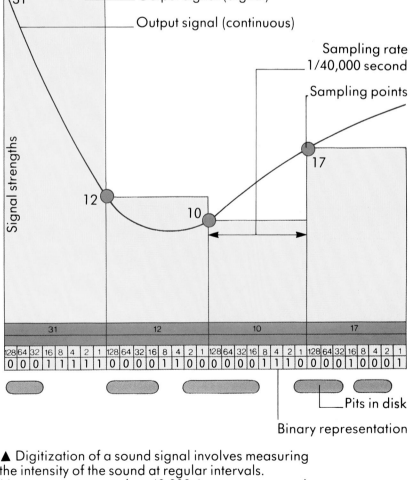

▲ Digitization of a sound signal involves measuring the intensity of the sound at regular intervals. Measurements are taken 40,000 times every second. Each value of sound intensity is converted into a binary number, a string of zeros and ones. These numbers are recorded on the disk by cutting small pits in the disk to represent a zero or a line of zeros.

Part Two

The computer age

Computer technology is at the center of a new Industrial Revolution which has transformed modern life. The miniaturization of electronic components is one reason for the enormous growth in computing in recent years. Computers of all types, from the home computer to the giant mainframe, are becoming more powerful. They are also able to perform many new functions. Computers are at work helping scientists and artists, musicians and engineers. Computers are vital in banking, and control the movements of huge sums of money around the world. They supervise the flight of aircraft and spacecraft, and they store information for governments. Computers are used in medicine to display the internal structure and condition of patients' bodies. In schools and colleges the computer is helping to train the next generation of computer users.

◀ The intricate circuitry of a computer circuit board, which carries the electronic components that make the computer work. The circuitry itself is designed with the help of a computer.

Computer basics

● A "megaflop" is one million floating-point operations per second. The fastest modern supercomputers operate at speeds of thousands of megaflops.

● The ENIAC computer of the 1940s used so much electricity that the lights of Philadelphia dimmed when it was switched on.

● Work is in progress in Japan to produce a "fifth generation" of computers that would use "artificial intelligence."

▶ Using a home computer. Computers are increasingly used in the home as well as for running the operations of many businesses and industries. In the home they are used for entertainment and education; they also store information such as addresses, telephone numbers, and the family accounts. Computers as word processors are also increasingly popular.

Computers are machines that can perform three important functions. They can both store and recall information which is fed into them. The information is put into the memory of the computer and can be brought back from the memory when it is needed. They can also process that information according to certain instructions. The instructions can be fed in from the outside in the form of a computer program. Both the information and the program must be given to the computer in a form that it recognizes. Computers are becoming more powerful as it becomes possible to build smaller and smaller electronic components.

Fast workers

Computers can store information and process information. The two measurements which are used to describe the performance of a computer are therefore its memory capacity and its processing power. Memory is measured by the number of "bits" of information that can be stored. We shall see later that a "bit" of information has a precise meaning. Processing power is measured by the number of instructions or arithmetical or logical operations that the machine can carry out in one second.

Computers that have a large memory capacity are used for storing information such as personal details, vehicle licenses, tax liabilities, and much other data concerning millions of people. The information is stored in a "database" which allows it to be updated and sorted as required.

Many computers in industry are used to monitor a particular process and take certain actions depending on what they measure.

▶ The American space shuttle has five on-board computers which monitor and supervise the flight. The race into space was long a main driving force behind the development of computing power. The first astronauts used computers less powerful than many home computers today.

These programs are called "expert systems" because they are replacing skilled and experienced human operators. Computers with large processing power are used for performing mathematical calculations at high speed. Many of the world's most powerful computers are used to forecast the weather. Machines which generate moving pictures on screen for various purposes also need large processing power.

Systems and programs

A computer must be able to both store information and process it. All the information, or data, is stored in binary code. Each word or number is represented by a sequence of ones and zeros. These are stored in the main memory in electronic charge-storing devices called capacitors. A one is represented by a charged capacitor, a zero by an uncharged capacitor.

Many thousands of capacitors are arranged in rows and columns, so that each one has a grid reference number called a location address. Each capacitor is attached to a transistor, which acts as a switch. By switching on a particular transistor, the computer either can find out whether a one or a zero is stored at a particular address, or can change what is stored. These two processes are called reading and writing.

When the data have been read, they pass to the central processing unit (CPU), which also reads instructions from the memory. The CPU contains an arithmetic and logic unit, which can add, subtract, multiply, and divide or compare numbers read from the memory.

Programs

Computers receive their instructions from two types of program. The operating system program gives the computer fundamental rules on how it is to work. This program is sometimes stored in a read-only memory (ROM), which cannot be changed. The instructions which tell the computer what to do can be written by the computer user and entered into the computer memory. These programs will be stored in the random access memory (RAM), along with the stored data. Any part of this memory can be read from and "written to" as required.

Programs have to be written in a language that the computer recognizes. There are many different computer languages, each suitable for certain applications. To run a program, the computer has to translate it into a sequence of simple operations. These are reading from a memory address, adding or comparing two numbers, or writing to a memory address. This sequence of steps is programmed using "machine code."

Computer languages

Programmers use a variety of different languages to write programs. A popular language for beginners is called BASIC. More advanced languages include FORTRAN, PASCAL, and COBOL. The children in the picture (left) have used a language called LOGO to program a so-called "turtle" to draw geometric shapes.

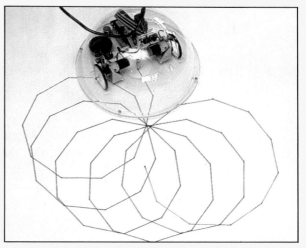

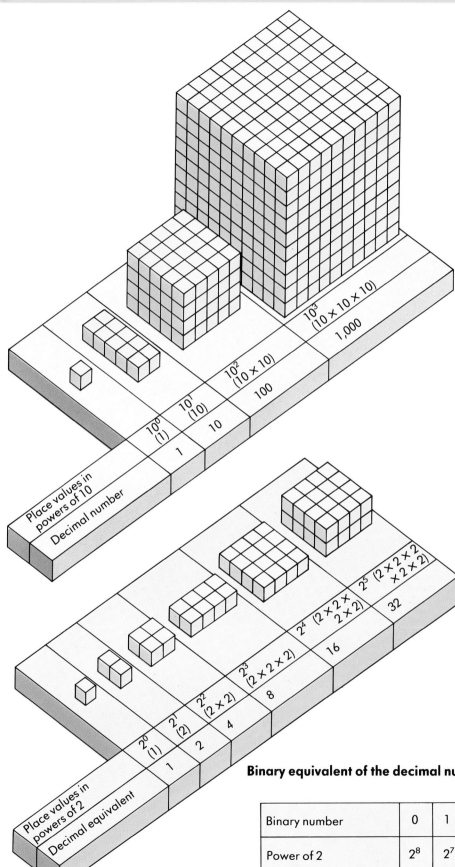

The decimal system

Our ordinary number system is based on ten numbers, or digits: 0, 1, 2, 3, ..., up to 9. It is therefore known as a decimal, or base-10, system. Numbers larger than 9 are expressed in digits using the idea of place values: the value of a digit depends on its place in the number. Place values go up in powers of ten, as illustrated on the left. (Any number to the power zero is one.) The number 153 therefore breaks down to 1×10^2 plus 5×10^1 plus 3×10^0.

Decimal number 153

Sample number	1	5	3
Power of 10	10^2	10^1	10^0
Equivalent decimal number	100	10	1

The binary system

The earliest computers carried out operations using decimal numbers. But today's computers use a number system based on two, the so-called binary system. In this system only two digits are required to express a number, the binary digits ("bits") 1 and 0. In a computer these two digits can be simply represented as, for example, the flow (1) or nonflow (0) of electric current. As in the decimal system, the binary system builds up numbers using place values. In binary the place values go up in powers of 2, as illustrated on the left. The table below shows the binary equivalent of 153.

Binary equivalent of the decimal number 153

Binary number	0	1	0	0	1	1	0	0	1
Power of 2	2^8	2^7	2^6	2^5	2^4	2^3	2^2	2^1	2^0
Equivalent decimal number	256	128	64	32	16	8	4	2	1

Microcircuits

Computers contain a very large number of switches. They are used to allow access to each element of the memory, and also to perform the arithmetic and logic functions of the CPU. The size and weight of a computer depends on how small the switches can be made.

The modern computer can be made so small because it uses switches of microscopic size, known as transistors. These are linked in miniature electronic circuits along with other microscopic components, such as capacitors. Using such microcircuits, the entire CPU and memory of a powerful computer can take up only a few square centimeters.

Transistors and the other microcomponents are made from silicon. Silicon is a semiconductor, a material with electrical properties between a conductor and an insulator. Crystals of silicon can be made to conduct electricity a little when impurities are added to them.

A transistor is made of three layers of silicon, which have had different types of impurities added to them. The central layer, called the base, is treated (or "doped") with a different impurity from the upper and lower layers.

These are called the emitter and the collector. Small changes in voltage between the base and the emitter can switch on and off relatively large currents between the emitter and the collector. This control is very sensitive, and switching uses little power.

The microscopic components of computers are not made separately and then connected together externally. They are formed, along with the circuits that link them, within a single wafer-thin crystal, or chip, of silicon. This arrangement is known as an integrated circuit.

Hundreds of identical chips are manufactured at the same time from a round slice of silicon. The slice goes through a lengthy series of masking, etching, and doping operations to create the three-layer electronic components and circuits on the chips. Masks are designed hundreds of times larger than lifesize and then photographically reduced. After manufacture, which must take place in the cleanest possible, dust-free environment, each chip is tested by probes, and the faulty ones rejected. The good ones are mounted and wired on plastic blocks for connection to external circuits.

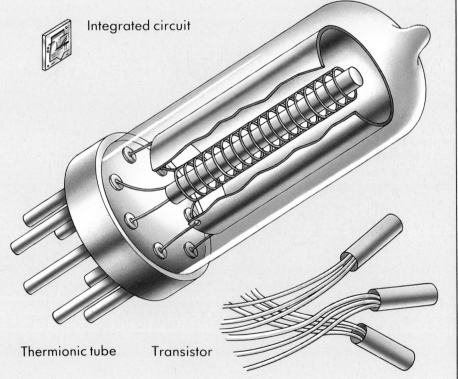

Shrinking circuits

In the 1830s the English inventor Charles Babbage designed, but never built, a mechanical computer, called the Analytical Engine. The modern computer was born when the necessary switching became electronic, in the form of electron tubes. The first electronic computer was built at the University of Pennsylvania in 1945. Called ENIAC (Electronic Numeral Integrator and Calculator), it used over 18,000 tubes and occupied a large room. Computers became very much smaller in the early 1960s because they used tiny transistors instead of tubes. Within a decade, computers had shrunk even more because of the introduction of integrated circuits on silicon chips. The shrinkage still continues: more than 1 million components can now be squeezed into each square centimeter (less than 1/6 sq. in.) of chip.

Integrated circuit

Thermionic tube   Transistor

▶ A very close look at the surface of an integrated circuit. In a computer, information is stored in binary code, as a series of the binary digits (bits) 0 and 1. Each bit is stored in miniature capacitors. If the capacitor is charged, that represents 1; if it is uncharged, that represents 0. The charge in the capacitor can be changed by the switching action of transistors. The transistors are turned on and off by voltage lines which run across them.

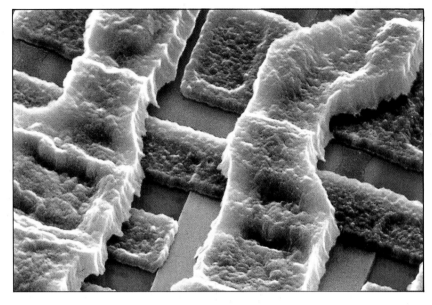

▼ A magnified picture of an integrated circuit in the jaws of an ant. Computer designers are constantly trying to produce smaller and smaller components and connections. This allows more computing power for the same area of circuit board.

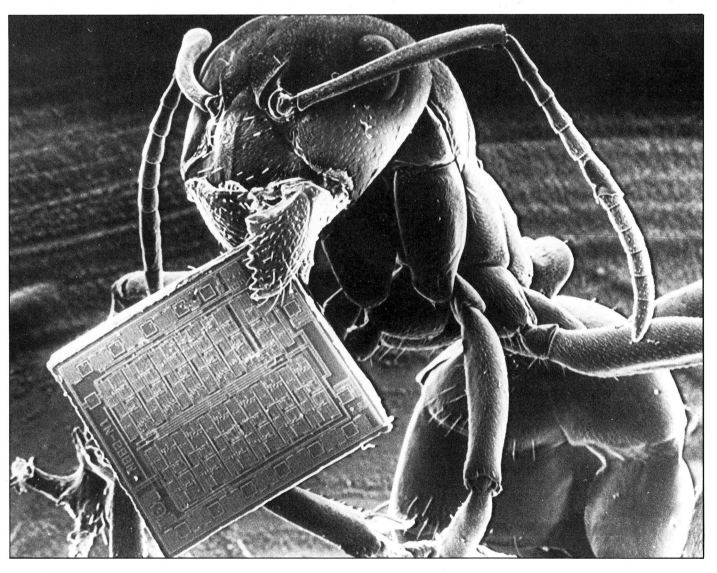

Micros and mainframes

Spot facts

• The world's first 16-megabit (16 million bits) microchip was produced in 1990. The memory was stored on a chip the size of a fingernail.

• If the fuel efficiency of the automobile had increased at the same rate as computer technology, it would run for 5 million kilometers (3 million mi.) on 4.5 liters (just over a gallon) of gasoline.

• It took the personal computer just ten years to catch up with the mainframe in terms of sales. From 1977 to 1987, sales rose to $28 billion from nothing.

Microprocessors and computers have caused a revolution in business, travel, and communications. Microcomputers are available in many schools. Industry and commerce rely on them more and more. The power of the computers we use is increasing rapidly. A personal computer today can be as powerful as the largest computer in the world was 20 years ago. The rate of advance continues at an astonishing pace. Mainframe computers can now perform up to billions of calculations in one second. No doubt even this extraordinary speed will be increased greatly in the future, as computers become more powerful.

▶ A view inside a mainframe computer. This is the Cyber 205 supercomputer. It can carry out millions of arithmetical calculations every second. The wiring is extremely complex, and the operation of the computer generates a high temperature. Future computers may use laser beams instead of wires to carry information.

Pocket calculators

Mechanical calculating machines first came into use in the 1600s. Early digital machines were built by the mathematicians Blaise Pascal in France and Gottfried Leibniz in Germany. They carried out calculations by means of rotating wheels. But mechanical calculators became obsolete with the introduction of electronic devices based on the silicon chip. The first pocket calculators appeared in 1970.

Pocket calculators have a keyboard, a processor, and a display. The processor is an integrated circuit. It contains circuits which interpret the signals from the keyboard, circuits which power the display, and two types of memory. One memory is used to temporarily store numbers or instructions; the other is for permanent storage of programs which can calculate the answer.

This is how the calculator works if the operator wants to multiply 9 × 13. When the number 9 key is pressed, the processor stores the binary code for 9, which is 1001, in its display memory. It also shows the number 9. When the × key is pressed, the processor remembers that, and also copies the display memory to another memory location, called the operand register. When 1 is pressed, the 1001 is replaced in the display memory by 0001 and the display shows 1. When the 3 is pressed, the 0001 is moved into a second display memory cell, and the first cell contains 0011. The display shows 13. If the = key is now pressed, the processor will multiply the number in the operand register by the number in the display memory and will display the answer.

Most calculators have a liquid crystal display (LCD). Behind the front screen of the display each position where a number can be shown is divided into eight segments. Seven straight-line segments are used to show all the numbers, and one circular segment can be used to show the decimal point. Each segment contains a substance which can affect the properties of light passing through it. Behind all the segments is a mirror. When the display is off, light from outside passes through the liquid crystal, reflects from the mirror, and goes back through the liquid crystal. The display is uniformly illuminated. When a small voltage is applied to the liquid crystal in a segment, it stops the light from being reflected and the segment appears dark. The shapes of numbers are built up in this way. LCDs require so little power that many calculators are powered by solar cells.

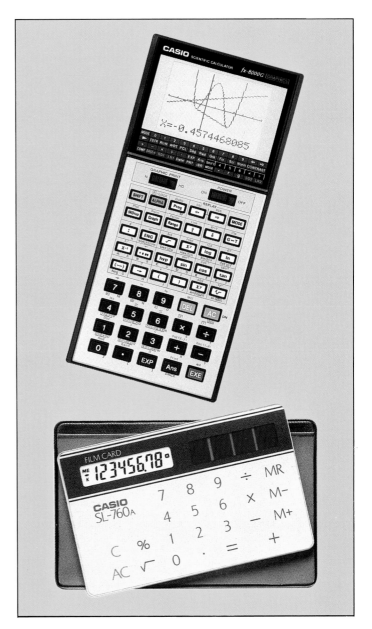

▶ Many different types of pocket calculators are now available. They vary in size and complexity. Small and simple is the so-called "credit-card" calculator (bottom), which is similar in size to a credit card. This model has simple arithmetic functions. It is powered by a set of solar cells. By contrast the scientific calculator (above) has multiple functions, including logarithms and trigonometric values. It also has a large liquid-crystal display, on which quantities can be expressed graphically. It is powered by batteries.

The microcomputer

Microcomputers are used in all areas of business and industry, in banks, stores, and offices, in the home, and in schools. Knowledge of computers is becoming more and more important in almost all types of work. There were particularly rapid advances in microcomputers in the 1980s because of progress in the manufacture of integrated circuits.

A microcomputer consists of a small number of chips, arranged on a printed-circuit board. Each chip is made for a particular job within the computer. The most important chip is the microprocessor. This chip contains all the circuits for performing the calculations of the computer and for checking the answers to the calculations. Other chips on the circuit board provide the basic memory of the computer: the ROM and the RAM. The capacity of a computer is usually expressed in terms of its RAM. A small home computer might have a RAM of 128K. K stands for kilobytes, or thousands of bytes; one byte equals eight bits.

A clock chip sends out electrical pulses to various parts of the computer to ensure that events happening at different places on the circuit board are synchronized.

Peripherals

The microcomputer also contains circuits which control the flow of information into and out of the computer. These are called input/output (i/o) ports. All the devices from which the computer receives instructions, or to which it gives instructions, have to be permanently attached to the computer or plugged into an i/o port. Such devices are called peripherals.

The keyboard is an important source of input information for the computer. In some home computers the microprocessor is inside the keyboard.

Storage capacities compared

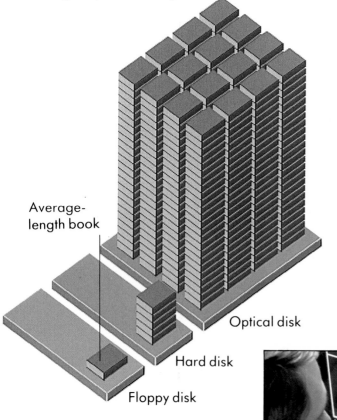

Average-length book

Optical disk

Hard disk

Floppy disk

▲ The capacities of the different kinds of disks used to store computer data vary enormously. An optical disk can store hundreds of times more information than a high-capacity floppy, magnetic disk, and dozens of times more than a small hard disk. It typically stores information in the same way as the compact disk, as a series of pits in the disk surface, which can be "read" by a laser.

▼ An engineer working with a microcomputer on a design project. He is using a "mouse" to make changes to the design he has created in color on the screen. Computer-assisted design (CAD) has become one of the most valuable engineering research tools.

Programs and data may be stored on magnetic tape or floppy disk. The information is recorded in the magnetism of crystals in the tape or disk. Floppy disks are made of flexible plastic. There are two standard sizes: 5¼ inches (133 mm) and 3½ inches (88 mm). The recordings run in circles, or tracks, on the surface. To read the disk, it is put into a disk drive, where it is rotated beneath a sensor called a head. A hard disk is built into some computers and provides much greater storage capacity than a floppy disk.

The most important output device for a computer is the monitor. This is a screen like a television screen which displays the results of the computer's calculations. The display could show words, numbers, or pictures. The monitor also produces sounds for the computer. The monitor can display the output from the keyboard or disk drive, which allows the programs to be written and finalized on screen before the computer is asked to print them. Some monitors allow a computer to be controlled from a touch-sensitive screen.

Peripherals

▼ Inputs to the computer can come from many different devices. The joystick lever can be moved to give direction and speed instructions, usually for a computer game. The light pen can be used with a light-sensitive monitor to point to a particular position on the screen to give instructions. The mouse can be used to move a marker on the screen called the cursor. The cursor moves in the same direction as a ball beneath the mouse.

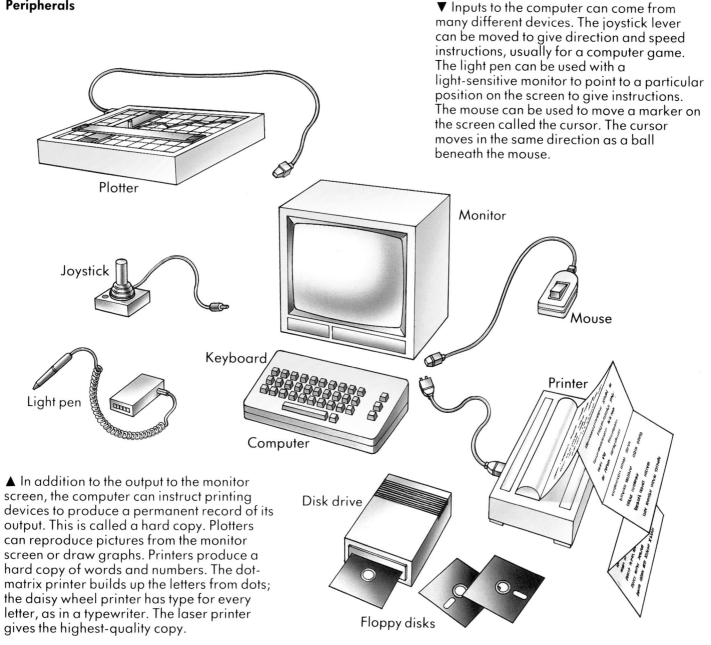

Plotter

Joystick

Light pen

Keyboard

Computer

Monitor

Mouse

Printer

Disk drive

Floppy disks

▲ In addition to the output to the monitor screen, the computer can instruct printing devices to produce a permanent record of its output. This is called a hard copy. Plotters can reproduce pictures from the monitor screen or draw graphs. Printers produce a hard copy of words and numbers. The dot-matrix printer builds up the letters from dots; the daisy wheel printer has type for every letter, as in a typewriter. The laser printer gives the highest-quality copy.

Microsystems

The microcomputer can form the nerve center of an extensive interacting system. The various inputs and outputs can measure and control operations, make inquiries, and respond. Some methods of entering information into a computer, such as the keyboard or mouse, need a human operator. However, the microcomputer can also be set up to monitor a process or activity continuously. It can be programmed to take certain actions in response to its measurements. Computers are widely used in the chemical industry in this way. They control the quantities of the chemical substances being used, the temperature and pressure at which reactions are taking place, and the properties of the end product.

All the measurements from instruments in the factory are converted to low-voltage signals that the computer can read. The computer measures the voltage on each of its input lines in turn. If any signal is low or high compared with the numbers in the program, the computer sends control signals to the machines in the factory to correct the problem. The computer control system can run day and night with no need for supervision or rest.

▶ The microcomputer can communicate with many devices attached to the computer. However, using a device called a modem (modulator-demodulator) it is possible for a computer to communicate with distant machines by using a telephone line. The modem allows the computer to send and receive messages from other computers. This is called electronic mail. It is also possible for a computer to search central libraries of information called databases. There are many methods of storing computer instructions and data. The hard disk, the floppy disk, and the cassette all use magnetic material. With an optical disk, words and numbers are stored as a series of ones and zeros by, for example, forming a small pit to represent a zero. The disk is read by laser. Optical disks are generally "read-only" – the information is permanent.

Joystick

Keyboard

Inpu

Lightpen

Buffer

Modem

Database

Network of other micros

Electronic mail

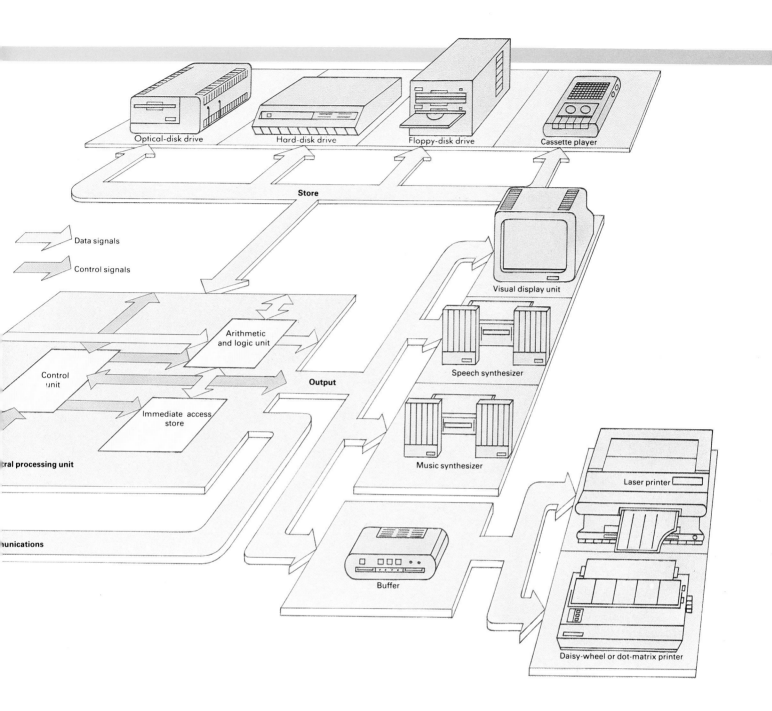

Optical-disk drive

Hard-disk drive

Floppy-disk drive

Cassette player

Store

Data signals

Control signals

Arithmetic and logic unit

Control unit

Immediate access store

Output

ral processing unit

nunications

Visual display unit

Speech synthesizer

Music synthesizer

Buffer

Laser printer

Daisy-wheel or dot-matrix printer

In order to read voltage signals from monitoring devices, a computer must be fitted with an analog-to-digital (A/D) converter. The voltage measurement is an analog signal; this means it can take any value and can change smoothly. The computer can understand only a digital signal which can be represented in binary code, and must therefore be a whole number. An 8-bit A/D converter produces the 256 binary numbers between 0 (00000000) and 255 (11111111) for an input voltage of 0-5 volts. So a measurement of 3.70 volts produces the binary number for 3.70 multiplied by 256/5, which equals 189.44. Rounded down, that is 189 (10111101).

Buffers
Computers can send out information to other devices at an extremely high rate: up to 19,000 or more bits per second. The receiving devices may be unable to cope with the speed of the computer. It is necessary to install a unit called a buffer between the computer and the receiving device. The buffer stores the information from the computer and then sends it out at the rate that the device requires. Because the computer works so quickly, it can interact with many devices, apparently at the same time, by constantly checking all the devices to see if any of them is waiting for instructions.

The mainframe

The largest and most powerful computers are called mainframes. They are used as the central data storage and processing machines for large corporations and government departments. Many other smaller computer terminals can be connected to the mainframe and all use its huge processing power.

Mainframe computers are also used to solve problems which require a vast number of calculations. One of the most complex of these is the prediction of weather based on the information gathered at weather stations. Many different physical properties form part of the calculation, such as temperature, humidity, wind speed, and air pressure. All these aspects of the weather affect the others according to the laws of physics. These are fed into the computer as mathematical equations. The computer calculates how each of the properties will change in the short term and then uses these new values to predict those for the long term.

The fastest mainframes or supercomputers can do more than hundreds of millions of arithmetical operations (add, subtract, multiply, divide) a second. The processing power of a computer is measured in "flops," or "floating-point operations." One hundred million of them would be called one hundred megaflops.

Computers of this speed consume a great deal of electrical power. A major consideration in their design is how to regulate the rise in temperature generated in their operation. Some supercomputers are cooled by liquid.

There is much research being carried out into making computers even faster. "Parallel processing" allows the computer to perform many calculations at the same time in different parts of the machine. The optical computer may one day increase speeds by using light instead of electricity within the machine.

► A Cray machine at the U.S. National Supercomputing Center, at the University of Illinois. The computer uses parallel processing to calculate at incredible speeds, counted in billions of operations per second.

▼ A three-dimensional image generated by a powerful mainframe computer in a nuclear reseach laboratory. It shows an "event" taking place inside an electronic particle detector. The event is a collision between a proton and an antiproton, producing an electron (blue) and other particles, such as neutrinos.

▲ A modern mainframe computer room. Because of the miniaturization of electrical components, computers have become much smaller. As a result, housing them has become easier. In the early days of mainframes, it was important that computer rooms had good air conditioning and sensitive temperature controls. Such restrictions are fewer with today's mainframes. Computer storage in this computer room is on magnetic tape, stored in plastic reels. This method is bulky, and storage may in the future move to a more compact medium.

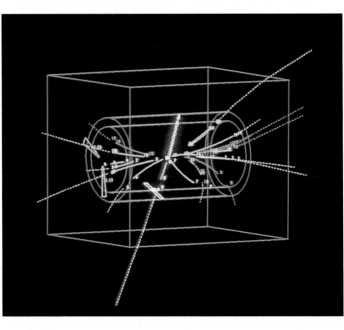

Computers at work

During the 1980s computers in business and industry grew from a rarity to an essential feature of commercial life. They bring great advantages, but also some dangers. Information can be stored compactly on disk and retrieved easily, but a damaged disk can lose volumes of records. A computer memory is more easily lost than a book, or other record system on paper. Computers can communicate with each other, but this allows outsiders to gain access to the information. Updating of records is easy, but tampering and erasing are also easy. Security of computer-based records is an important and difficult problem in today's business.

► Modern video game machines use advanced microprocessors to draw and move the graphics on the screen. Using computers, even in an arcade, is a useful experience for future employment. However, too much time spent with only a computer for company can make people addicted and antisocial.

Simulators

A simulator is a computer-controlled machine which artificially produces the sights, sounds, or movement of a real-life situation. Simulators are used to train people to respond properly to the real event.

Computer simulators and fast-action video games both rely on the ability of the computer to generate pictures and to update them quickly enough to produce the illusion of continuous motion. The speed and complexity of computer graphics has increased rapidly because of the desire of the military, aviation, and space agencies to improve the effectiveness of training simulators.

Flight simulators for aircraft are essential for pilot training because of the huge risk and cost of having untrained pilots flying real aircraft. Two computers control the simulator. One operates hydraulic pistons, which lift or roll the cockpit in response to the controls. The other generates the view which the pilot sees. The computer memory contains a map of the training area, which it displays and moves according to the movement of the simulator controls.

The most recent simulators for military aircraft contain highly detailed pictures of potential target areas. The computer can also simulate different weather conditions and create lighting appropriate for day or night. The displays for simulators have to fill the trainee's field of vision to be convincing. Lasers are used to draw the computer-generated pictures on a large screen. Another display method is to produce the image on a small screen which is incorporated into the trainee's helmet.

▼ A trainee pilot of the Swiss Air Force practicing an approach to an airfield using a flight simulator. The view which the pilot sees is computer-generated and changes in response to the controls which the pilot uses. The cockpit also is moved by a computer to respond as if it were a real aircraft.

Computers in education

The use of computers in education has increased dramatically over the past ten years. Computers are now available in many classrooms for all ages of children and adults involved in learning and teaching. For young children, the computer is a source of entertainment as well as learning. Programs are available which can help children read and write. The computer will show a picture of an object or animal and ask a question about it. The child has to be able to read the question, think about the answer, and tell the computer. This is done by moving a marker to the correct answer from alternatives shown on the screen; by typing the answer, correctly spelled; or, in the case of the most advanced teaching machines, by speaking to the computer.

Computers as word processors are used extensively in education, for schoolchildren and university students. The advantages of the word processor are so great that writers of all kinds are now using them. Students, teachers, journalists, and novelists all rely on the computer in place of the typewriter or the pen. A spelling-check program can educate or merely correct mistakes, depending on the willingness of the user to learn.

▼ Computers are now used by many children at school and at home. Because the increase in the use of computers is so recent, children are often more familiar with them than their parents. The training that children receive on computers, even from playing games, will help them in their future working lives in an increasingly computerized world.

Software has been developed which allows students with a microcomputer to learn at their own pace, and follow their own course. The program presents the student with some information and a choice of which aspect of the subject they want to know more about. The student chooses, and that information is displayed with another choice for further related study. Entire encyclopedias are available on disk, containing pictures, sounds, film, and copies of contemporary documents. Any of these can be chosen by selecting from a choice of symbols (called icons) displayed on the screen. Moving pictures are stored compactly by recording only the differences between one frame and the next. On videotape the whole picture is recorded for every frame.

Computers are used to teach foreign languages. The computer can show a piece of writing on screen in any language. It can ask for a translation of a word and correct any mistakes. It can ask the student to choose which of a choice of words best fits into the text at a particular place. Computer programs have not yet been developed which can teach a spoken language.

An important use of computers is to teach the use of computers. Programs exist which guide students through the process of writing computer programs. The program can monitor what is being written and point out mistakes or parts of the program which could be improved. But the main purpose of computers in schools is to give students practice in using them.

▼ Computers can help us communicate. The girl (inset) is using a computer which recognizes her speech when she responds to its questions. The boy (main picture) cannot move his hands, but he can use the computer by speaking into the microphone.

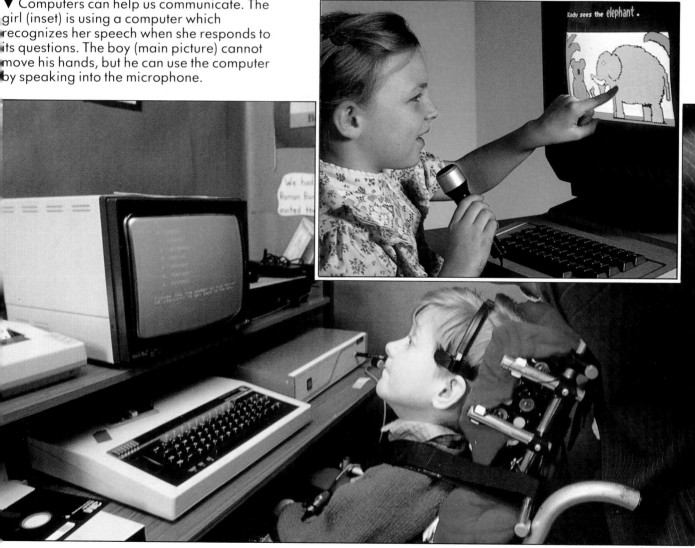

Computers in finance

Banks have been using computers since the invention of the electronic calculating machine in the 1950s. They have continued to use computers and automated electronic systems as the technology has become more advanced.

The use of computers most obvious to customers is in the automatic banking machines installed at most banks. Customers can withdraw cash or find out how much is in their account from the bank's records.

Many banks have joined networks which allow a customer of a member bank to withdraw money at any other bank belonging to the network. This system requires that the computers of each bank be able to exchange information. They must be compatible. When a customer takes out money, the computers ensure that the correct amount is deducted from the right account at the right bank.

Most international banking is now done by computer. Electronic signals travelling over telephone lines can transfer funds from one bank to another and from one continent to another. Billions of dollars are moved around the world every day by computer. Great care must be taken to keep the system secure. The computer programs which control financial business are greatly concerned with security. They must ensure that any instruction to release money is genuine.

Computers have had enormous impact on the stock exchanges of the world. At a stock exchange, dealers buy and sell stocks in corporations. This used to be done by people with stocks to sell talking to those who wished to buy. Now stocks can be transferred by computer. Dealers use personal computers in the office to show them the current prices of all the stocks. Prices may be colored red or blue depending on whether the price is going up or coming down. When stocks are bought or sold, computers transfer the ownership of the stocks and the money of the buyer. Computers can be programmed to buy or sell stocks automatically when the price reaches a certain value. On bad days, many people blame the automatic nature of the computerized system for the rapid fall in stock prices.

▶ The Hong Kong Stock Exchange. Each worker has a computer terminal, a printer, and a telephone. Nearly all communication with the outside world is electronic.

▲ A cash dispenser allows access to money 24 hours a day. Users have a plastic card and a personal number to identify themselves to the machine.

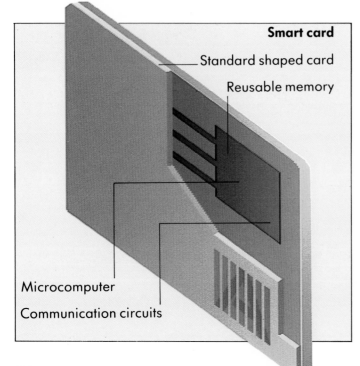

Smart card

Standard shaped card

Reusable memory

Microcomputer

Communication circuits

◀ A "smart" card is the size of a credit card but instead of a strip of magnetic tape it has a microcomputer inside it. When used to pay for purchases, the value of the goods is automatically deducted from the value of the card.

Computers in the office

Office work is the area of business which has been most influenced by the computer and the microprocessor. Secretarial work in particular is dominated by the use of the word processor in place of the typewriter. Printers, photocopiers, and fax machines all contain microprocessors to control their operation.

The word processor consists of a keyboard and a screen, or display. The letters and numbers of the keyboard are laid out in the same way as on a typewriter. The text is typed in and displayed on the screen. The words can easily be changed and moved about.

The word processor can display any part of a long document, move sections of text around, change layout, produce bold, underlined, or italic script, all without any retyping. When the text is complete, it can be sent to a printer, which puts the text on paper.

Local area network
Letters or documents need no longer be filed in paper form. They can be filed electronically in the word processor's memory. Standard documents can also be stored there. When they are needed, they are brought on the screen. Names, dates, or other information specific to the new document are inserted where necessary. It can then be printed.

In big companies large and small computers are used to carry personnel records, calculate and print out payroll information, and so on. In manufacturing industries, computers often control the purchase of equipment and materials, ensuring that the materials arrive at the right time. In sales and marketing departments computers hold lists and order requirements of customers.

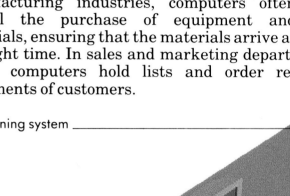

Scanning system _____

Personal computer _____

▶ The modern office contains an integrated system for its information technology. Personal computers on every desk can exchange information with a central computer or with peripheral devices such as scanners, copiers, and printers. The system of inter-connections between the devices is called a local area network.

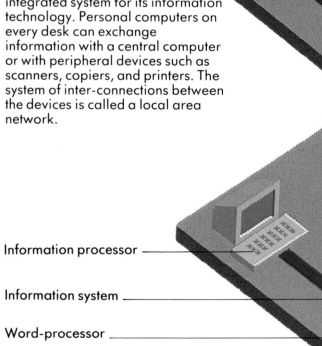

Information processor _____

Information system _____

Word-processor _____

◀ Specialist computer systems are invaluable in design offices, as here. Using the keyboard or a "mouse" to input data, designers can easily compose and alter plans and pictures on screen. Designs can then be sent to customers via a modem and telecommunications links, or they can be faxed: sent by facsimile transmission.

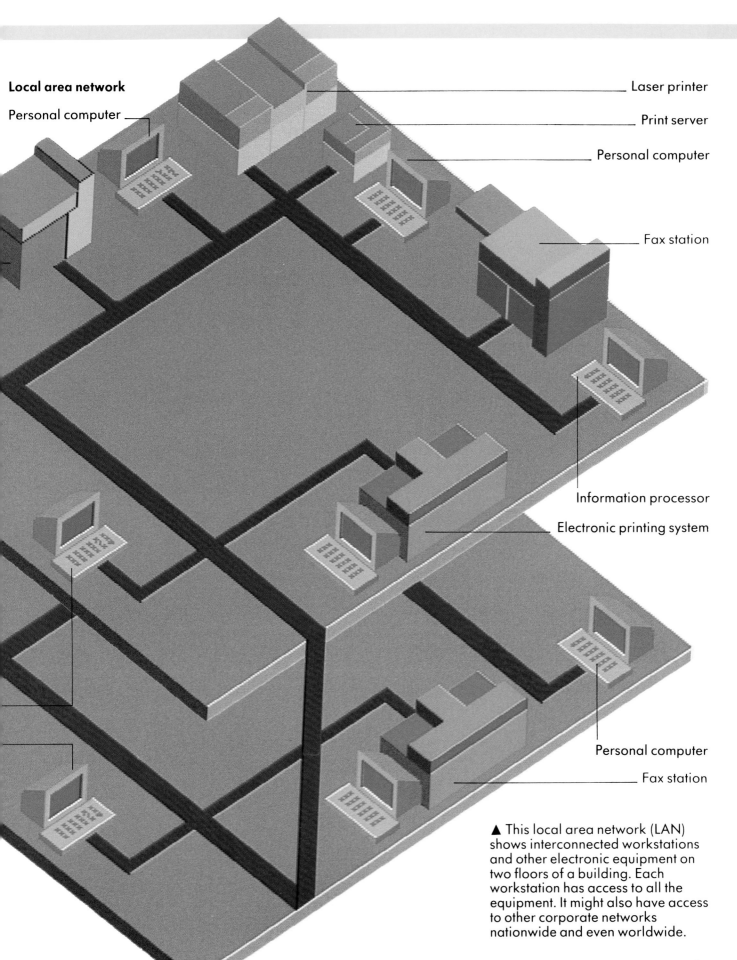

Local area network

Personal computer

Laser printer

Print server

Personal computer

Fax station

Information processor

Electronic printing system

Personal computer

Fax station

▲ This local area network (LAN) shows interconnected workstations and other electronic equipment on two floors of a building. Each workstation has access to all the equipment. It might also have access to other corporate networks nationwide and even worldwide.

Designing with computers

Spot facts

- *Computer-aided design (CAD) could one day reduce the number of design engineers by 80 percent.*

- *The first CAD video game was a simple black-and-white tennis game called Pong. It was invented by Nolan Bushnell, founder of the Atari company, in 1972.*

- *High-resolution computer monitors can display over a million points on the screen. This is roughly five times the resolution of a standard color TV.*

- *The computing power required to store video information is daunting. An ordinary floppy disk can store only enough data to generate a tenth of a second of video film.*

▶ A three-dimensional picture of a chemical molecule displayed on a computer screen. The image may be moved and viewed from any angle. Research scientists use the computer picture to understand the properties of a molecule. Biochemists use it to design molecules for particular tasks.

Everything that people make, from buildings and automobiles to pictures and music, has to be designed. Designing is a creative process which starts with human imagination. Successful design results in creations which accomplish the intended result in exactly the desired way.

Some computer programs are written to assist with design. With this new tool, designers can try out far more ideas than could be examined before. They can also quickly find answers to problems that previously took far too long to solve. Computers can extend the creative powers of engineers, scientists, artists, and musicians.

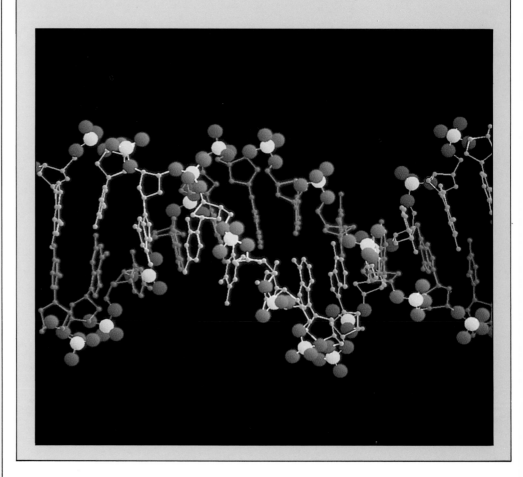

Making music

Music is constructed from many different elements. The most important ones are rhythm and harmony, though there are many more. Composing music is an artistic process and, like all the arts, it has its own set of rules to guide the artist toward pleasing results. These rules are by no means rigid, and most composers break them.

The idea of using machines to compose is not new. A composing machine belonging to Samuel Pepys, who lived in London in the 1600s, still survives at Magdalene College in Cambridge. Computers are good at following instructions, and programs have been made which incorporate the rules of musical composition. They can also introduce some random variations to produce a different result each time. A computer was first used to compose a piece of music in 1955. Music composed by a computer is not as popular as music from a human composer. This may be because computers are unable to mimic human artistic ability, or because we do not have programs sophisticated enough to compose well.

Synthesizers

Synthesizers are complex pieces of electronic equipment which combine a musical keyboard with a computer. A musical note has three distinct phases. In the "attack" phase the sound builds up; it then stays roughly constant, and then fades during the "decay" phase. The characteristic way in which a note goes through each of these phases gives each instrument its own distinctive sound. A synthesizer can adjust each of the phases independently, and so can produce sounds which copy different instruments. The computer produces the music played on the keyboard so that it sounds as though it comes from the chosen instrument.

▼ The contemporary band Kraftwerk, from Germany, uses synthesizers extensively in its music. The musicians program the synthesizers to produce exactly the sound they want. This may be varied while they play the keyboard. Interesting music is a blend of sounds, some following and some breaking the rules of harmonic theory. Bands like Kraftwerk use a computer to produce some of the music but use their talents to compose other parts.

Artistic design

The process of skillfully and imaginatively creating a new and often attractive object is called art. Computers now assist in many branches of commercial art. Graphic designers use computers extensively to plan their work. Typically, such programs allow the artist to rough out a design on the screen, trying out colors, altering lines and text at will. During the designing process, the artist may move elements about and change the picture as often as necessary. When the work is satisfactory, it can be printed out. To do this, another program converts the numbers which created the image on the screen into the string of instructions necessary to drive a color plotting machine.

Textile designers use a similar method to allow their customers to view patterns without the need to produce fabric. Once the plotted pattern is agreed upon, the computer generates the sequence of instructions necessary to drive a weaving machine, and the pattern is automatically produced.

Computers are also used to renovate valuable old paintings. Details of the painting are first entered into a computer as a very long string of numbers representing the color at each point in the picture. The program already has a knowledge of how different renovation techniques affect each color. The computer then calculates how the painting would look if a particular renovation technique were used on it. The renovator selects the best process.

Computers also assist the cosmetic industry. Exact color production is very difficult but becomes extremely important where makeup is concerned. Computers help beauticians define and produce exactly the shade they want.

▼ An artist (below left) painting with computer graphics, using the screen as his canvas. He selects a color from the multi-hued "palette" on the right of the screen and directs it to the desired place in his picture. A beautician (below right) uses a computer-aided design program to picture realistically the effects of different colors of makeup.

Computer graphics provide many new opportunities for artists. The "palette" from which a computer artist can select colors allows for any shade to be moved easily and quickly. Areas of the picture may be repeatedly colored over and still appear fresh, and there is no waiting for paint to dry. The computer can produce a string of new pictures exactly like the original. Each one can then be altered slightly, so that when replayed in sequence, they give the impression of continuous movement. This technique is called computer animation.

Computers can also be used to produce abstract artistic patterns. Such programs contain rules which produce a variation in color over the picture. There are no programs that actually make up a picture the way an artist does. As with music, this is not because computers cannot physically do what is necessary, but because people cannot write down what instructions must be followed in order to produce an original and pleasing result.

▲ A graphics designer uses a computer and "paint" software to experiment with different patterns and colors to create unusual visual effects.

▼ Computer graphics programs give commercial artists new dimensions. It enables them, for example, to create unusual typefaces for advertisments.

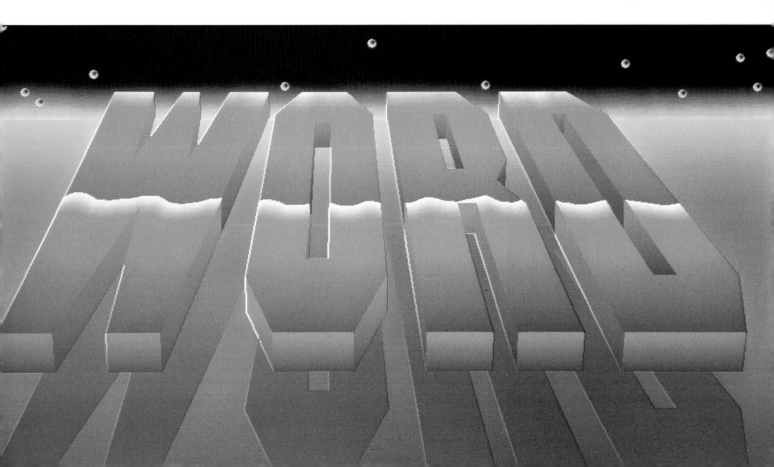

Computer imaging

Computers can be used to display as a picture the measurements taken in experiments. The picture is much easier to understand than the long string of numbers used to make the picture. This is called computer imaging. For example, the experimental measurements might be the amount of rainfall at different places in a country or the intensity of X-rays passing through different parts of a patient's body. The results are shown as a map.

Usually a color code is used to show areas at which similar results were obtained. The changes in color show the variations in the measured values. The presentation of the measurements as a multicolored picture can immediately give an impression of the shape and sometimes even the motion of objects invisible to the human eye.

Computer-imaging techniques are required to display pictures of the ground taken by remote-sensing satellites, such as *Landsat*. The satellite records electronically the intensity of reflected light at a number of wavelengths, and sends back signals that computers process into false-color images.

A computer display can be used to picture things which cannot be photographed. For example, astronomers measure the intensity of invisible radiation, such as radio waves coming from stars, and use a computer to display the results. The results of radar detection of aircraft or of weather formations are also displayed on a screen.

Computers are also used to interpret sounds used in underwater detection. Sound waves are sent down from a surface vessel. The strength of the echo is measured, and the results are displayed as a map of the seabed. This method can detect sunken ships and was used to find the *Titanic*. It has also been employed in the underwater search for the legendary Loch Ness monster in Scotland.

▼ A computer-generated image of the intensity of the light coming from different parts of the galaxy called M51. The computer displays the measurements as a three-dimensional picture. Brighter points on the photograph are shown as higher peaks. The variations in intensity are color-coded to increase the clarity of the picture.

Computer imaging is extensively used in hospitals to create pictures of the inside of a patient's body. These reveal internal problems without the need for an operation. High-frequency sound called ultrasonic sound is used to provide pictures of unborn babies inside their mothers. Doctors can check that the baby is developing properly.

Radio waves are used to study the chemicals in the human body by magnetic resonance imaging (MRI). The patient lies inside a large cylindrical magnet. In a magnetic field, atoms are able to absorb radio waves of a certain frequency. Different atoms absorb different frequencies, so the concentration of each kind of atom can be measured within the body.

Another powerful imaging method is called computerized axial tomography (CAT) scanning. A flat beam of X-rays spreads out from a source, passes through the patient, and is detected behind the patient. By rotating the X-ray source, the section of the body being examined can be viewed from every angle. A computer then composes a complete picture.

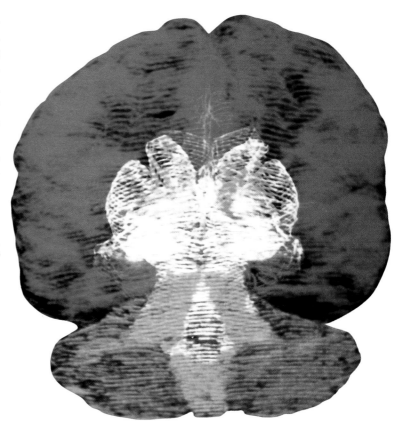

▼ A kaleidoscopic false-color image of the Newquay area of Cornwall, England, produced by computer-processing data acquired by a Landsat satellite. It shows the patchwork pattern of fields in various hues. The prominent linear feature in the middle of the image is the runway of Newquay airport.

▲ A picture of a human brain as seen from behind. Different areas of the brain are assigned colors by the computer. The red areas represent the hemispheres of the forebrain, which control thought, memory, sight, and language. The orange areas control balance and muscle movement.

Molecular modeling

Molecules are built up of atoms. There are only about one hundred different types of atoms, but they can be combined in countless different ways to form a huge variety of molecules. Strict rules govern the ways in which atoms may combine with each other. This means that computers can be programmed to model them.

Researchers into molecular structure often know which atoms are present in a molecule, without knowing the molecule's shape. Many of the chemical and biological properties of a molecule depend crucially on its shape. A computer may be used to examine the possible molecular structures, which it does by applying the rules of atomic physics. The computer can suggest the most probable shape for the molecule.

Doctors who are doing research into the causes of disease often use biochemistry to isolate the particular molecules which are responsible. They can then produce a computer model of the molecular shape. Using the computer again, they can design new molecules which have the right shape and properties to interfere with the effects of the harmful molecule. These programs give doctors an important tool to help their search for new drugs and treatments for illness.

▼ A computer-generated image of the influenza virus. The central core contains the virus's DNA. The projections on the virus help it break into a healthy cell. Once inside the cell, the virus reproduces rapidly. The computer modeling of the virus can help in the design of chemicals to restrict the damage it can do.

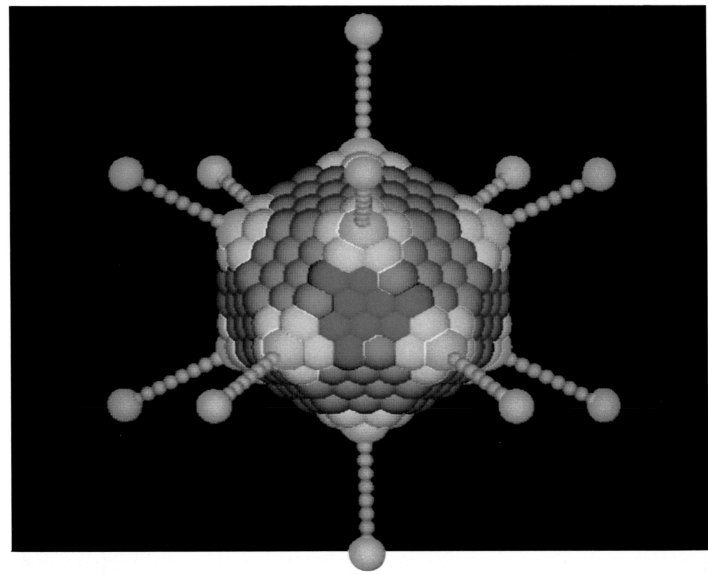

The modeling and display of large biological molecules such as proteins requires enormous computing power. The relative positions of thousands of atoms have to be given to the computer. Each different type of atom is shown in a different color and a different size. The computer then calculates which atoms are in the foreground and which are partly hidden by other atoms. Finally, on each atom the computer adds shading to make each circle appear to be a sphere.

▼ Scientists now use computers to study the molecules of existing compounds and to help them design new ones. The molecules are imaged in 3D and can be modified on the screen (inset). The main picture shows an image of a molecule of hemoglobin, the substance that gives blood its red color.

Viruses that cause diseases such as influenza and AIDS can be visualized using computer modeling. The models help doctors to design vaccines against viruses. Unfortunately, viruses change, so that within a few years it may be necessary to design a new vaccine against the modified virus.

Computers can help in understanding molecular structure by automating experiments and analyzing results. The molecule which is the basis of genetic material is called DNA. Many people are working on the analysis of human DNA, which consists of a long chain of many millions of small molecules of only four different types. Discovering the exact sequence of these four molecules would take thousands of years to achieve without computers.

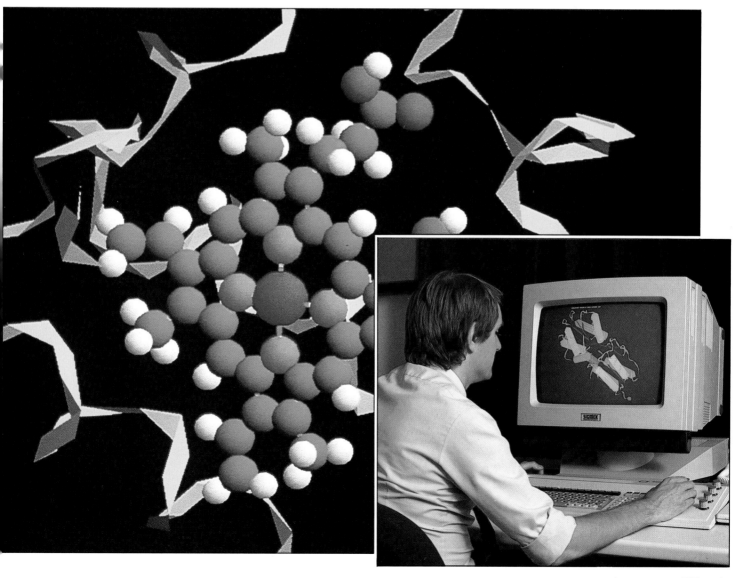

Computer-aided design

Engineers imaginatively create appealing new devices which fulfil their desired function. This process involves calculations, examination of alternatives, and the analysis and presentation of solutions. Computer-aided design (CAD) assists engineers in all of these tasks.

CAD programs usually allow the engineer to enter into a computer a representation of the design through a movable hand-held device called a mouse. The program converts the designer's instructions into numbers, which are processed to represent the object on a screen. There are CAD programs which allow this picture to appear to be in three dimensions (3D). The engineer may view the device from any angle and so have a very clear idea of how the object will look and work. When satisfied with the concept, the engineer must produce detailed drawings and a component list so that the device can be made. Two-dimensional programs are used for this, and take their inputs either from 3D programs or directly from the designer.

Computer-aided design programs on desktop computers have replaced the drawing board completely in many industries. When these drawings are completed on screen, another program is used to convert the numerical representation of the drawing into instructions for a printing machine to follow. Other programs are used to analyse the components, and predict how each will behave. For example, the movement in a structure carrying a load can be calculated. A program can plot the way in which heat or electricity will flow through a component, and show how much it will cost to make.

It is possible to integrate several CAD systems with manufacturing machines to form a complete process from design to production. Examples of this are rare because of the expense and complexity of introducing it, but in some industries it may be necessary for commercial success. Car manufacturers in Japan, for example, already use such systems. Designers produce sketches of an idea, from which detailed drawings are produced. The computer uses its knowledge of existing parts, supplies, and machines to produce a program of work necessary to make the design. When a machine is ready to produce each component, the system gives the necessary sequence of instructions directly to the machine. When all the parts have been prepared, the computer informs the engineers, who may then arrange for assembly. The use of computer-aided design programs cuts down the cost of product development. It reduces the number of prototypes which have to be made and then scrapped because they are not quite right.

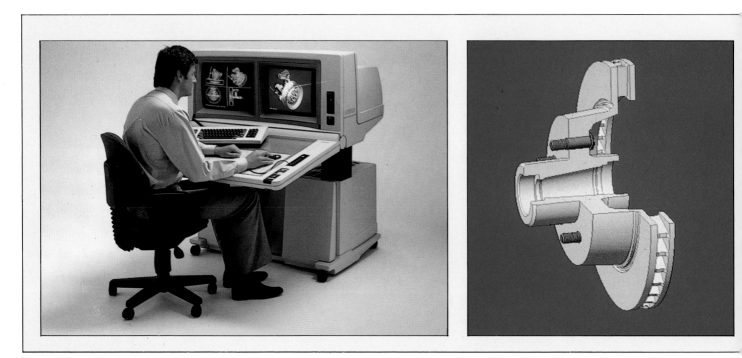

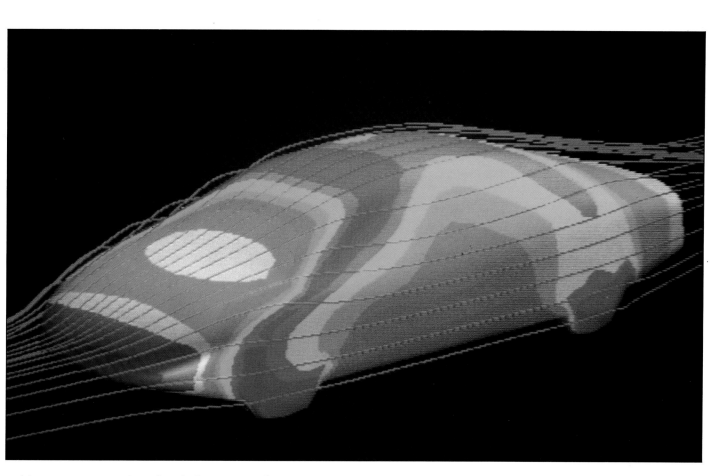

▲ New cars are analyzed with CAD to produce an optimal body shape. Here, a complex computer imaging package takes the results of a large design program and displays how air will flow over the car. Colors show how fast the air is flowing at the car's surface and hence how aerodynamic is its shape.

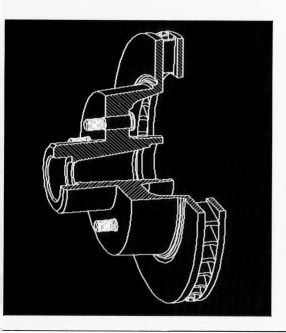

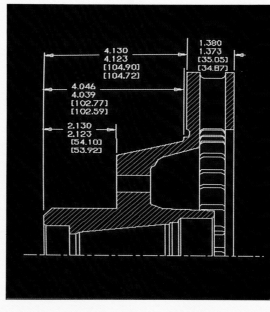

Engineering CAD

This disk brake rotor assembly is first drawn as a profile. The computer displays it from all angles. The operator can alter one measurement, and the computer changes all the others to match. It adds shading to make the drawing look more solid. All the measurements are stored in the computer's memory and can be used as a pattern.

Robot control

Spot facts

● *Robotized trains run in the San Francisco Bay area of California (BART). At peak times, 100 computer-driven trains run at high speed with only a 90-second interval between them.*

● *The automatic pilot of an aircraft is a typical "invisible" robot. An airplane may be landed by automatic pilot with a chance of failure of one in ten million.*

● *In 1988 there were 175,000 industrial robots in Japan. There were less than half that number in the rest of the world.*

● *The earliest kind of robot was a water clock, called a clepsydra, which was invented by Ctesibus of Alexandria, Egypt, about 250 BC. It recycled its water by means of a siphoning device which ran automatically.*

▶ *This Japanese robot has been taught to play an electronic organ. In its head is a television camera which enables it to see where the keys are so that it can direct its fingers to the right notes on the organ.*

A robot is a machine that can be instructed to perform tasks which would otherwise have to be done by people. Most robots have computer "brains," which can be programmed by an operator to carry out specific tasks. The latest robots are equipped with sensors which enable them to see, hear, touch or even smell their surroundings. They have an electronic brain sophisticated enough for them to decide how to act in response to this data. Hundreds of thousands of robots are now at work, and in the future, with advances in computer technology, robots will have even more complex "brains," which will enable them to learn from experience.

Automation

Before 1920 no one had ever heard of robots. The word was coined by the Czechoslovakian playwright Karel Čapek, from the Czech words "robota," meaning slave labor and "robotnik," meaning slave. In his play *R.U.R.* (Rossum's Universal Robots), robots were intelligent, hard-working, human-shaped machines which rebelled against their human masters and killed them when the robots were used for making war. Since then robots have appeared in many books and films, sometimes as good and helpful, but often as evil and destructive.

It is their ability to be instructed which distinguishes robots from machines that imitate human actions by mechanical means. Two thousand years ago, the Greeks and Romans could make statues that moved by hydraulic power. In the 1700s and 1800s there were life-size clockwork models which could even write and play musical instruments. However, these were only mechanical toys, and the correct name for them is "automata."

As long ago as 1804, the French engineer Joseph Marie Jacquard invented a loom which could be programmed to weave different patterns in silk cloth. This was done by inserting one of a series of stiff cards punched with holes into the loom. The card prevented some rods from carrying thread into the weave of the cloth while allowing others to pass through the holes. There were 400 of these warp threads altogether, so that very intricate patterns could be created. A revolutionary feature was that one machine could follow many different programs. Equally, many machines could be programmed to produce identical patterns. This was the first industrial automation.

In the 1950s machines came into use that could operate automatically, following instructions on punched paper tape or magnetic tape. These and later computer-controlled machines ushered in increasing automation in industry, bringing about a second industrial revolution. In the last few decades tireless computer-controlled robots have taken their place alongside human beings on factory production lines.

▼ A robot artist demonstrates its versatility at an industrial exhibition in Japan. That country boasts more robots than the rest of the world put together.

Designing robots

The human body is like a superbly engineered machine controlled by an incredibly complex computer: the brain. It will be a long, long time before robots are capable of responding to their environment, learning from experience, and thinking creatively with the dexterity of the human brain. Arms and hands are the human limbs whose functions are most often duplicated by robots. To have the necessary freedom of movement, robot arms, like human ones, have joints capable of moving independently of one another, up and down, side to side, and in and out. Robot arms can do some things better than ours, such as picking up heavy objects with ease, or rotating their "wrists" in a full circle.

The robot must be given a computer "brain" which will assess the difficulty of the task it has been given and decide how to set about achieving it. Suppose that a robot needs to pick up an object from a conveyor belt and place it in a box (a relatively simple task for a human).

To do this it needs an electronic "eye" to identify the object; if the object is not lying in the expected position, the "eye" relays this information to the computer, which reacts by instructing the arm to approach the object from a different angle to pick it up.

Many of today's robots can use "feedback." This is the ability to make decisions which depend on information about changing conditions. We have nerves to carry instructions from our brains to our muscles. Robots have electronic cables which transmit instructions from the computer to its motor-driven parts.

It is rare for robots to walk upright on two legs. This is because walking on two legs involves lifting one foot from the ground at every step, and becoming unstable. To give a robot the balance and coordination necessary to walk on two legs would take up a wasteful amount of space in its computer brain. So most mobile robots move on wheels, or on four or six legs.

▼ To hold this egg without breaking it, the robot hand needs information about the egg's weight and the fragility of its shell. Sensors transmit this information to the robot's computer "brain," which controls the strength and precision of the hand's movements.

▼ Pictured here are the plans and parts needed to build a robot arm and hand. There are sensors to gather information about the outside world, mechanical parts for the arm itself, and the connections to the controlling computer.

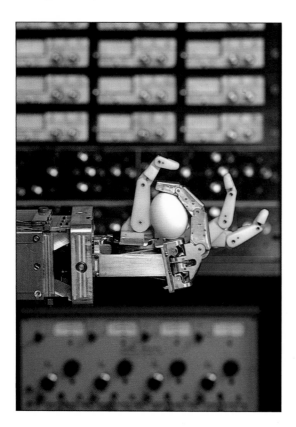

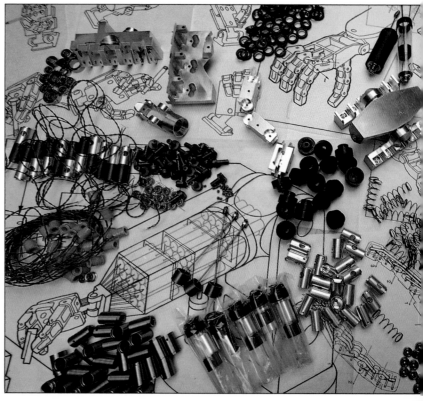

▼ A cutaway drawing of a one-armed industrial robot of the "pick-and-place" type. It is flexibly jointed so that it can move in three dimensions. It can swivel on its base; it can extend and retract its arm and move it up and down. Its gripper mechanism can pick up and release objects, pivoting and swiveling if need be. Each "limb" and joint of the robot is powered by compressed air, acting through pistons. In this way it can mimic many actions of the human body but, unlike that organism, can work continuously without tiring.

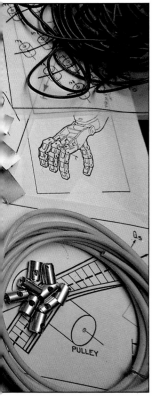

PULLEY

Robots at work

Robots now do many jobs which used to be done by people. They are particularly useful at industrial jobs which are repetitive, boring, or unpleasant. Examples are riveting and welding in assembly plants, and spraying paint on car bodies. Robots are better at this sort of job than people, because they can always work at the same level of precision and accuracy, and they never tire. Their work is therefore always of the same quality, and they can do more of it because they do not need rest breaks.

Robots can also do jobs which are dangerous for human beings. They can handle radioactive materials in nuclear power plants, or toxic chemicals, without needing protective clothing. They can also work in environments which would be too hot or too cold for humans. They can be used where a human life would be at risk, such as in disarming bombs or searching for explosives, and of course in space.

Robots are ideal for space work because they do not need air to breathe and never grow old. Robots are used to carry out maintenance work on Earth satellites and to travel to distant planets for purposes of exploration and discovery, like the *Voyager* space probes.

Robots as care givers

An increasing number of robots are being used as domestic help, particularly to provide services for physically handicapped people. A robot helper can enable handicapped or frail elderly people to live alone, independently of their families, and this saves them having to move into a hospital. Research is now being carried out, particularly in Japan, to develop robots capable of giving safe nursing care to sick or elderly people, and this is expected to be an area of rapid growth in the near future for a new generation of very intelligent robots.

▶ A robot waiter serves food in a restaurant in California. Robots are already perfectly capable of performing simple domestic tasks like this. Robots are now being developed for more complex and demanding work, such as the care of the elderly and handicapped.

▼ An artist's impression of the *Voyager 2* space probe approaching the planet Uranus in January 1986. The probe transmitted its observations back to Earth as radio waves via the dish antenna, which had been programmed always to point in the right direction.

Units of measurement

Units of measurement

This encyclopedia gives measurements in metric units, which are commonly used in science. Approximate equivalents in traditional American units, sometimes called U.S. customary units, are also given in the text, in parentheses.

Some common metric and U.S. units

Here are some equivalents, accurate to parts per million. For many practical purposes rougher equivalents may be adequate, especially when the quantity being converted from one system to the other is known with an accuracy of just one or two digits. Equivalents marked with an asterisk (*) are exact.

Volume
1 cubic centimeter = 0.0610237 cubic inch
1 cubic meter = 35.3147 cubic feet
1 cubic meter = 1.30795 cubic yards
1 cubic kilometer = 0.239913 cubic mile

1 cubic inch = 16.3871 cubic centimeters
1 cubic foot = 0.0283168 cubic meter
1 cubic yard = 0.764555 cubic meter

Liquid measure
1 milliliter = 0.0338140 fluidounce
1 liter = 1.05669 quarts

1 fluidounce = 29.5735 milliliters
1 quart = 0.946353 liter

Mass and weight
1 gram = 0.0352740 ounce
1 kilogram = 2.20462 pounds
1 metric ton = 1.10231 short tons

1 ounce = 28.3495 grams
1 pound = 0.453592 kilogram
1 short ton = 0.907185 metric ton

Length
1 millimeter = 0.0393701 inch
1 centimeter = 0.393701 inch
1 meter = 3.28084 feet
1 meter = 1.09361 yards
1 kilometer = 0.621371 mile

1 inch = 2.54* centimeters
1 foot = 0.3048* meter
1 yard = 0.9144* meter
1 mile = 1.60934 kilometers

Area
1 square centimeter = 0.155000 square inch
1 square meter = 10.7639 square feet
1 square meter = 1.19599 square yards
1 square kilometer = 0.386102 square mile

1 square inch = 6.4516* square centimeters
1 square foot = 0.0929030 square meter
1 square yard = 0.836127 square meter
1 square mile = 2.58999 square kilometers

1 hectare = 2.47105 acres
1 acre = 0.404686 hectare

Temperature conversions

To convert temperatures in degrees Celsius to temperatures in degrees Fahrenheit, or vice versa, use these formulas:

Celsius Temperature = (Fahrenheit Temperature − 32) × 5/9
Fahrenheit Temperature = (Celsius Temperature × 9/5) + 32

Numbers and abbreviations

Numbers

Scientific measurements sometimes involve extremely large numbers. Scientists often express large numbers in a concise "exponential" form using powers of 10. The number one billion, or 1,000,000,000, if written in this form, would be 10^9; three billion, or 3,000,000,000, would be 3×10^9. The "exponent" 9 tells you that there are nine zeros following the 3. More complicated numbers can be written in this way by using decimals; for example, 3.756×10^9 is the same as 3,756,000,000.

Very small numbers – numbers close to zero – can be written in exponential form with a minus sign on the exponent. For example, one-billionth, which is 1/1,000,000,000 or 0.000000001, would be 10^{-9}. Here, the 9 in the exponent -9 tells you that, in the decimal form of the number, the 1 is in the ninth place to the right of the decimal point. Three-billionths, or 3/1,000,000,000, would be 3×10^{-9}; accordingly, 3.756×10^{-9} would mean 0.000000003756 (or 3.756/1,000,000,000).

Here are the American names of some powers of ten, and how they are written in numerals:

1 million (10^6)	1,000,000
1 billion (10^9)	1,000,000,000
1 trillion (10^{12})	1,000,000,000,000
1 quadrillion (10^{15})	1,000,000,000,000,000
1 quintillion (10^{18})	1,000,000,000,000,000,000
1 sextillion (10^{21})	1,000,000,000,000,000,000,000
1 septillion (10^{24})	1,000,000,000,000,000,000,000,000

Principal abbreviations used in the encyclopedia

°C	degrees Celsius		kg	kilogram
cc	cubic centimeter		l	liter
cm	centimeter		lb.	pound
cu.	cubic		m	meter
d	days		mi.	mile
°F	degrees Fahrenheit		ml	milliliter
fl. oz.	fluidounce		mm	millimeter
fps	feet per second		mph	miles per hour
ft.	foot		mps	miles per second
g	gram		mya	millions of years ago
h	hour		N	north
Hz	hertz		oz.	ounce
in.	inch		qt.	quart
K	kelvin (degree temperature)		s	second
			S	south
			sq.	square
			V	volt
			y	year
			yd.	yard

Glossary

A/D converter (analog-to-digital converter) A device which converts signals from measuring devices such as voltage meters into the digital information which a computer requires.

air pressure The force exerted by the air. It reflects the density of air molecules at a particular point in space. Sound waves are variations in air pressure which move through the air.

AM (amplitude modulation) A system of carrying sound signals on a radio wave by varying the amplitude (height) of the radio wave.

analog signal A smoothly varying signal such as a measurement of a smoothly varying physical property such as air pressure or time. The opposite of a digital signal.

animation Computer animation involves using a computer to produce a series of pictures which give the impression of continuous motion when they are shown in quick succession.

antenna An electrically conducting device which can intercept radio or television waves in the air and pass them to an amplifier and loudspeaker.

aperture The hole behind the lens of a camera which allows light to fall on the film. Decreasing the size of the aperture increases the depth of field but also increases the required exposure time.

arithmetical operation A process of addition, subtraction, multiplication, or division.

bandwidth A range of frequencies. The range required to carry the information for a radio, telephone, or television signal.

BASIC (Beginners All-purpose Symbolic Instruction Code) A computer programming language in which many of the instructions are English words. Because of this simplicity, it is usually the first computer language which people learn.

binary code A simple code in which all letters and numbers are represented by a string of numbers, each of which is either ONE or ZERO. Binary code is used by computers because it can be easily converted into the ON or OFF state of a string of electrical switches.

bit (binary digit) A single unit of information in binary code. A ONE or ZERO in a number string or the ON or OFF of an electrical switch.

buffer A device which takes information at high speed from a computer and passes it on to another device such as a printer at a speed which the slower device can handle.

byte A string of binary digits that a computer processes as a unit. Usually a group of eight bits.

C An advanced computer-programming language.

CAD (computer aided design) Using a computer to assist engineers in mechanical or electrical design. The computer can be used to visualize design, test compatibility between components, and produce finished drawings of the design.

camcorder The name sometimes given to a camera which records onto a video cassette. The name is a shortening of "camera recorder."

capacitor A component which can store electrical charge.

carrier frequency The fundamental frequency of the electromagnetic wave which is used to carry a radio, telephone, or television signal through the air.

cathode A negatively charged electrode. The positive electrode is the anode. Electrons will flow from the cathode to the anode.

cathode-ray tube The central component of a television. A beam of electrons is directed toward a screen where a chemical coating gives off light at the point which the beam hits. The beam direction can be rapidly changed by varying the voltage on electrodes on each side of the electron beam.

cellular telephone A local communication system in which each small area, or cell, is served by its own radio transmitter. Communication between cells goes via a central control computer.

chip A single semiconductor circuit manufactured on a piece of silicon. Many identical circuits are made at the same time on a large wafer of silicon. The individual circuits are then chipped off and packaged.

chrominance signal The information on how much of each of the colors red, green, and blue should be shown at each point of a TV screen.

clock chip A part of the computer which produces a regular timing signal. The signal ensures that all processing and transfer of information is done at the right time, and in the right order.

communications satellite A relay station in space which detects, amplifies, and retransmits communication signals between distant points on the Earth's surface.

compact disk An information storage system which has replaced magnetic tape in many applications. The information is stored in binary code and is read from the surface of the disk by a laser.

complementary color A color and its complementary color are opposite to each other. When the two are added the result is either black (in printing or photography) or white (in a TV).

contact print A print made by placing a negative on a piece of film and then exposing the film to light through the negative.

CPU (central processing unit) The part of a computer which performs the calculations and comparisons between numbers.

daguerreotype One of the first types of photograph. It did not use film but exposed a picture onto a metal plate.

database A computer program designed to store a large amount of information. It allows easy access and cross-referencing between different data entries.

depth of field The range of distances from the camera which are brought into focus by the camera lens at one time. The depth of field is determined by the aperture size.

diaphragm A thin sheet of material which moves in response to variations in air pressure in a sound wave.

dichroic mirrors Mirrors which reflect some colors of light and transmit other colors. They are used to separate colors.

digital information Information expressed as a series of numbers.

digital signal Information which is expressed as a series of numbers, usually in binary code. The digital signal is obtained from a smoothly varying analog signal by measuring it at regular intervals, and taking the nearest whole number.

disk drive The device which spins the computer disk beneath a reading and writing head, and exchanges information between the disk and the computer.

doping Adding specific impurities in particular quantities to alter the physical properties of a material.

dot-matrix printer A type of printer which makes up each letter, or character, from a pattern of dots.

electromagnetic radiation Radiation which consists of oscillating electric and magnetic fields. This includes radio, X-rays, and visible light. Unlike sound, which needs air or another substance through which to travel, electromagnetic radiation can travel across completely empty space.

electron A negatively charged particle. The movement of electrons constitutes an electric current. Electrons are also a constituent of atoms.

electron tube A device for controlling the flow of electrons which contains an electrode from which electrons are given off. It may have a metal grid to which a voltage is applied. The voltage controls the flow of electrons. A change of voltage can produce a rapid change in the flow of electric current through the tube.

electronic mail or **e-mail** A system by which computers can be used to transfer information between themselves along standard telephone lines.

expert system A computer program which is specifically designed for a particular task and incorporates the experience and knowledge of experts in the field.

exposure time The length of time for which the shutter on a camera is opened. With a longer exposure time, more light will reach the film.

feedback Taking a signal from a system being controlled and returning it to the control mechanism. This allows the control mechanism to monitor the results of its actions.

flop (floating-point operation) A single arithmetical calculation.

floppy disk A disk of flexible magnetic material contained in a plastic or cardboard case. A cheap and portable way of storing information.

FM (frequency modulation) A system of carrying sound signals on a radio wave by varying the frequency of the radio wave.

focusing Adjusting a lens so that the image formed by the lens is as sharp and clear as possible.

FORTRAN (formula translation) A programming language used for scientific and mathematical problems.

frequency The frequency of a wave describes how many times it goes up and down in a second. Frequency is measured in hertz (Hz). One hertz is one oscillation per second.

galley A metal tray into which completed lines of typeset material are placed. When the page is complete, the galley is used to print from. This print is called the galley proof.

geostationary At a constant position above a particular point on the Earth's surface. Geostationary satellites have to be above the Equator and at a set distance nearly 36,000 km (over 22,000 mi.), from the Earth. This is almost one-tenth of the distance to the Moon.

graphics The ability of a computer to create pictures on a screen by controlling the color of each element of the area of the screen.

gravure A method of printing in which the printing plate contains many thousands of small indentations which hold the ink.

hard disk A disk for information storage which is permanently installed as part of the computer.

hardware/software The hardware is the machinery of the computer. The software is the program material.

hertz (Hz) The unit of frequency. One hertz is one oscillation per second. Sound waves are measured in hertz or kilohertz (one thousand hertz). Radio waves are in the range

10 kHz to over 100 MHz. One megahertz (MHz) is one million hertz. Visible light frequencies are about one billion megahertz.

imaging Using a computer to display a set of measurements as a picture.

infrared radiation Electromagnetic radiation having a wavelength longer than visible light but shorter than microwaves. Wavelengths in the range 0.7 micron (0.00003 in.) to 0.1 mm (0.004 in.).

integrated circuit A circuit manufactured in a multilayered piece of silicon by removing the silicon in each layer in a specific pattern. The remaining material acts as the components of the circuit.

i/o port (input/output port) A socket on the computer where data can enter or leave the computer along wires.

ionosphere Layers of the atmosphere which contain charged particles. They lie at a height of between 50 km (30 mi.) and 500 km (300 mi.) or more. The ionosphere is used to reflect radio waves back to Earth.

laser A device which can produce extremely intense, highly focusable beams of electromagnetic radiation. Most lasers give out visible light or infrared radiation.

laser printer A printing method which uses a laser to illuminate paper according to a particular pattern. The illumination determines the places where ink is put on the page and which areas are left blank.

letterpress A method of printing in which the letters to be printed are raised above the background. The raised surface is inked and paper is pressed against it.

logical operation A process of comparing numbers to determine, for example, if one is larger than

another. Computers can perform both logical operations and arithmetical operations.

luminance signal The information on the overall brightness of each point to be shown on a TV screen.

machine code The coded instructions which tell the computer in detail what to do. All computer programs have to be translated into machine code before any program can be carried out. The translation is done by the computer.

memory address The numbered locations within the computer memory at which bytes of information can be stored.

memory capacity The number of bytes of information which a computer can store.

memory cell The physical location of a bit of information within the memory.

micron A unit of length. One millionth of a meter.

microprocessor A single chip which contains a complete central processing unit.

microwaves Electromagnetic radiation having a wavelength longer than infrared radiation but shorter than radio waves. Wavelengths in the range 0.1 mm to 1 m (0.004 in. to 3 ft.).

modem (modulator-demodulator) A device which takes digital information and modifies it so that the information can be sent along a telephone line. At the other end of the line a second modem will extract the original information from the signal, presented as either words or pictures.

modulation The alteration of either the frequency or the amplitude of a wave.

movable type The printing technique of setting a page of type by

putting together separate metal letters to copy the page to be printed.

multiplexing Using a single cable or communication channel to carry more than one signal at a time.

negative A photograph in which the areas of light and dark are reversed. A bright area in the photographed scene produces a dark area on the negative. Color negatives contain the complementary color of the scene.

operating system The program instructions which start the computer running and which tell the computer how to interpret the instructions which the computer operator might use.

optical disk A means of storing information for a computer which closely resembles a compact disc storing musical information. The binary code may be machined into the surface of the disk and is read by a laser. Optical disks generally contain read-only memory.

optical fiber A thin strand of transparent material contained in a plastic sleeve. Light can pass along the fiber without being lost from the sides.

oscillation The oscillation of a wave is the increase and decrease of whatever the wave is made of. For a sound wave it is the air pressure which oscillates. For a light wave it is the electric and magnetic fields.

palette The range of colors which a computer can generate on a monitor screen.

parallel processing A method of speeding up the operation of a computer by performing more than one task at the same time.

PASCAL A computer programming language.

pentaprism A five-sided piece of glass positioned behind the viewfinder in a camera.

peripheral Any device attached to a computer. Plotters, monitors, and printers are peripherals.

phosphor A chemical coating on a TV screen which gives off red, green or blue light when it is hit by an electron beam.

photoconductive material A material which changes its ability to conduct electricity when it is exposed to light.

positive A photograph in which brightness and color are the same as in the photographed scene.

primary colors A set of colors from which all other colors may be produced. In painting and printing, the primary colors are red, yellow and blue. In television, the primary colors are red, green, and blue.

processing power The speed at which a computer can perform instructions or arithmetical or logical operations.

program A structured list of instructions which tell the computer what to do. The instructions must be precisely written in the programming language being used with all the spelling and grammar correct.

radio waves Electromagnetic radiation having a wavelength longer than microwaves. Wavelengths greater than 1 m (3 ft.).

RAM (random access memory) The part of the computer memory which is used for temporary storage of programs and data.

resistance A property of all materials which measures how well they conduct electricity.

ROM (read-only memory) A permanent memory used for programs, such as the computer operating system, which must never be erased or for data (as on an optical disk).

sampling The method by which digital information is created. A smooth signal is sampled many times a second. The range of possible values is divided into many small steps. The measured value of the smooth signal is rounded up or down to the nearest step. Using this method, a continuously changing signal is approximated by a string of whole numbers.

screening The process of changing an original photograph into one composed of millions of dots.

semiconductor A material which is neither a good conductor nor a good insulator. The electrical conductivity of a semiconductor is very sensitive to external conditions, which makes it possible to make electrical switches from semiconductors. By changing the external conditions slightly, the conductivity can be rapidly switched from bad to good.

silver halide The light-sensitive material in photographic film. The crystals of silver halide darken when they are exposed to light.

solar cell A power supply which runs off the light from the Sun. Solar cells are often installed in pocket calculators.

stylus A sharp needle, usually of synthetic diamond, used to detect the shape of the groove in a record.

sync pulse (synchronizing pulse) A timing pulse which is sent with a TV signal to ensure that the brightness, color, and sound information for each frame are kept together.

synthesizer A device which electronically generates sounds. By changing the details of how the sound is made, many different instruments can be imitated.

telegraph The long-distance transmission of simple information such as the dots and dashes of Morse code, or the movement of magnetic needles.

touch-sensitive screen A monitor screen which can be used to send instructions to the computer. The screen displays choices for the user and is sensitive to touch as the user points to the desired choice.

transducer A device which converts one form of energy into another. Many sensing and measuring devices are transducers. The device might measure a physical property and convert the measurements into an electrical signal.

transistor A device made from a semiconductor material which can act as a switch for electric current. A transistor consists of three sections, called the base, the emitter, and the collector. It can be controlled by a very small voltage applied to the base. Transistors are the basic computer components. They can be as small as a wavelength of light.

VDU (video display unit), or monitor The screen of a computer which can display graphic pictures, words, or numbers.

VHF/UHF/SHF Frequency ranges of radio waves: very high frequency, ultrahigh frequency, superhigh frequency.

vidicon A camera tube which measures the brightness at each point of an image focused on its surface.

wavelength The distance between successive peaks in a wave. Radio waves have a wavelength between a one meter (3 ft.) and a few kilometers. Visible light has a wavelength of less than one-millionth of a meter.

word processor A machine containing a microprocessor which runs a program designed to allow the efficient manipulation of words and text. Sections of a typed piece of writing can be moved, copied, or erased as required. The program enabling this to be done may also be called a word processor.

Index

Page numbers in *italics* refer to pictures. Users of this Index should note that explanations of many scientific terms can be found in the Glossary.

Further reading

Asimov, Isaac. *How Did We Find Out About Microwaves?* New York: Walker & Company, 1989.

Ault, Roz. *BASIC Programming for Kids*. New York: Houghton Mifflin Company, 1983.

Billings, Charlene W. *Fiber Optics: Bright New Ways to Communicate*. New York: Dodd, Mead, 1986.

Bitter, Gary G. *Exploring with Computers*. New York: Messner, 1983.

Cavanaugh, Ann. *The Computer Primer: A Complete Guide for Gifted Beginners*. Chicago: Childrens Press, 1984.

Darling, David J. *Computers at Home: Today and Tomorrow*. Minneapolis: Dillon Press, 1986.

Darling, David J. *Fast, Faster, Fastest: The Story of Supercomputers*. Minneapolis: Dillon Press, 1986.

Darling, David J. *Inside Computers: Hardware and Software*. Minneapolis: Dillon Press, 1986.

Darling, David J. *The Microchip Revolution*. Minneapolis: Dillon Press, 1986.

Darling, David J. *Robots and the Intelligent Computer*. Minneapolis: Dillon Press, 1986.

D'Ignazio, Fred. *Messner's Introduction to the Computer*. New York: Messner, 1983.

Dudley, Art. *Word Processing Basics*. New York: Prentice-Hall, 1985.

Elliott, Sharon. *Computers in Action*. New York: Bookwright Press/Watts, 1985.

Ford, Roger, and Oliver Strimpel. *Computers: An Introduction*. New York: Facts on File, 1985.

Graham, Ian. *Communications*. New York: Hampstead Press/Watts, 1989.

Hyde, Margaret O. *Artificial Intelligence*. Hillside, N.J.: Enslow Publishers 1986. (Revised edition of *Computers That Think?*, 1982.)

Irvine, Mat. *TV and Video*. New York: Franklin Watts, 1984.

Kettelkamp, Larry. *Computer Graphics: How It Works, What It Does*. New York: Morrow, 1989.

Lafferty, Peter. *More Science Projects: Communication*. New York: Marshall Cavendish, 1989.

LeBlanc, Wayne J., and Alden R. Carter. *Modern Electronics*. New York: Franklin Watts, 1986.

McKie, Robin. *Robots*. New York: Franklin Watts, 1986.

Nardo, Don. *Computers: Mechanical Minds*. San Diego: Lucent Books, 1990.

Pizzey, Steve, and Sheila Snowden. *The Computerized Society*. New York: Bookwright Press/Watts, 1986.

Schneiderman, Ron. *Computers: From Babbage to the Fifth Generation*. New York: Franklin Watts, 1986.

Wicks, Keith. *Working With Computers*. New York: Facts on File, 1987.

Picture Credits

b=bottom, t=top, c=center, l=left, r=right.

FSP Frank Spooner Pictures, London. MH Michael Holford, Essex. NASA National Aeronautics and Space Administration, Washington. NHPA Natural History Photographic Agency, Sussex. PP Picturepoint Ltd, Surrey. RF Rex Features, London. SC Spacecharts, Wiltshire. SCL Spectrum Colour Library, London. SPL Science Photo Library, London.

6 Zefa/Ted Horowitz. 8 The Ridgeway Archive. 9l RF. 9r, 10, 11 Zefa. 12l Mary Evans Picture Library. 12r Art Directors. 14 SCL/Muhlberger. 15l Bayerisches National Museum. 15r Ann Ronan Picture Library. 16 Kodak. 19t MH/Science Museum. 19b Minolta. 20l NHPA/S. Dalton. 20r SPL. 21 PP. 22 Sally & Richard Greenhill. 23l, 23r MH/Science Museum. 24l British Telecom. 24r Telefocus. 26 AT&T. 27t Telefocus. 27b John Price. 28 Robin Kerrod. 30 Sci Pix. 31 The Marconi Company Ltd. 32 John Walmsley. 33t PP. 33b SPL/Jerome Yeats. 35 Paul Brierley. 36 Zefa/Tom Tracy. 37l RF/Images by Goodman. 37r Sci Pix. 37b RF. 38 PP. 40t SCL. 40bl Ann Ronan Picture Library. 40br Peter Newark's Western Americana.

41 SPL/Dr. Jeremy Burgess. 42 PP. 43 Canon. 44l Sony. 44r Margaret Coreau. 46 Zefa/W. H. Mueller. 48 Zefa. 49 SC/NASA. 50l, 50r Sally & Richard Greenhill. 53t SPL/D. Scharf. 53b University of Liverpool. 54 Rainbow/Hank Morgan. 55t, 55b Casio Electronics Co. Ltd. 56l Imagine. 56r Zefa/Stockmarket. 60l Art Directors/W. Hodges. 60r SPL. 61 Woodfin Camp & Associates/M. L. Abramson. 62 Sally & Richard Greenhill. 63, 63 inset Rediffusion Simulation Ltd. 64 FSP/Mega. 65b Pete Addis/*New Scientist*. 65r SPL/Hank Morgan. 66l Imagine. 66r IBM/Eurocoor. 67 Art Directors. 68 IBM. 68-69 Imagine. 70 Chemical Designs, Oxford. 71l London Features International Ltd. 71r Pierre Mens/Press Promotion. 72l Central Office of Information. 30rSPL/Hank Morgan. 73t Pierre Mens/Press Promotion. 73b SCL. 74 SPL/Los Alamos National Lab. 75t SPL/Petit Format/B. Livingston. 75b SC. 76 SPL/Division of Computer Research & Technology, National Institute of Health. 77l, 77r Chemical Designs, Oxford. 78l Intergraph (G.B.) Ltd. 78r, 79bl, 79bt Applicon (U.K.) Ltd. 79t SPL/Hank Morgan. 80 FSP/Gamma. 81 SCL. 82, 82-83 Rainbow/Dan McCoy. 83 Sci Pix/Hall Automation. 84 NASA. 85 SPL/Lowell Georgia.